SCHWARTZEN PRECIL

BE YOUR OWN HERO

TURNING OBSTACLES INTO OPPORTUNITIES

www.heroleadershipgroup.com

ISBN-10: 1689026456

ISBN-13: 978-1689026451

Contents

Foreword

Twenty-six years ago, I lost my two youngest brothers to the foster care system. I tirelessly searched for them to no avail, but never gave up hope that one day I'd see them again - alive and well. Miraculously, they resurfaced into my life and brought with them: tales of resiliency in the face of insurmountable odds. "Be Your Own Hero" reveals the path that my youngest brother, Schwartzen, courageously embarked on from his earliest years of displacement and abuse, to his triumphant climb toward becoming an astonishing human being that I am very proud to call, "brother". It is a path best described as wān dào (弯道) or "winding road" of curves and sharp turns that disorients the wanderer, only to find themselves again - as a hero.

"Be Your Own Hero," challenges readers to awaken the hero within. Archetypal scholar, Joseph Campbell (as retold by Diane K. Osbon), describes the hero's journey as one's "willing to get rid of the life we've planned, so as to have the life that is waiting for us." Throughout these written chronicles, Schwartzen Precil's life unfolds with a vulnerability that wholly reminds us to embrace our transgressions and thwart becoming beholden to them. It is the emotional ingenuity of decoding life's internal puzzles that produces the magical thinking that inspires us and others, as Schwartzen valiantly shares.

What awaits you, the reader, is a stirring, thought-provoking discovery of how a young Black male, Haitian and Afro-Latine, survives ordeals meant to crush a child's imagination and darken their adult outlook on the world, but defiantly refuses to acquiesce. *Be Your Own Hero* takes its rightful place as a testimonial tribute to the enduring human spirit and belongs on the reading list of the self- motivated, the downtrodden, and the bold. Be bold in the journey to becoming your own hero.

Kalimah Priforce

P.S. Proud of you little brother.

Prologue

Parents are the initial foundation to the lives of their children. They are to provide comfort, stability, protection and guidance. Can you imagine what life might be like if you did not have your parents around? Unfortunately, this was the truth for my older brother and I as we were not fortunate enough to know our parents, be raised by them, or know anything about their whereabouts.

When I was a child, I told myself if I made it to the age of 25 and had no children to bear my name, I would write a book to my mother and family members whom I had never met. I would tell them the struggles I went through without having them around. I would also tell them how I overcame each of the challenge's life threw at me as a black boy growing up in foster care. With no parental guidance, I found solutions in different seasons along the journey of life.

A major fall out in a 10-year situationship was a rock bottom obstacle that fueled the search for the family I had never met. When I found my mother, I discovered there was more to my story than I ever imagined. I searched gruesomely for six months at 24 years old hungry to find the origin of my name. Drifting through life without my family's history enabled me to question everything about myself at any given moment. The first question I asked my mother when I heard her voice for the first time on April 30, 2019 was "where did my name come from?"

Most people who knew me personally knew my last name to be "Jarmond." That was my adopted name at the age of 14. When I saw my original birth certificate for the first time at 24-years-old I was blown away. I learned the story behind my name and changed my name back to my birth given name, Schwartzenegger Young Precil.

NOTICE OF CHANGE OF NAME
Notice is hereby given that an order entered by the Supreme Court, Erie County, on the 26th day of June, 2019, bearing Index Number 600312/2019, a copy of which may be examined at the office of the clerk, located at 92 Franklin Street, Buffalo, New York grants me the right to assume the name of Schwartzenegger Young Precil. The city and state of my present address are Buffalo, NY; the month and year of my birth are August, 1994; the place of my birth is Brooklyn, New York; my present name is Schwartzen Lormand Jarmond.
19-1124   jul8

"When you were in my womb," my biological mother explained in a thick Haitian accent, "I saw this man on TV. He was so strong and every time he was on TV, you (Schwartzenegger) moved in my belly. I knew you were going to be a strong man because that man on TV was very strong. I named you Schwartzenegger after 'Arnold Schwarzenegger.' He was a hero and you are my hero for finding me after all these years." My ears could hardly fathom the truth.

**

This book was my final attempt to find them. I wrote it in hopes that someone would recognize my face on the cover and point me in the direction of where my family was. Every important event in my life is documented within these pages and it started from a failed relationship with my foster parents, my significant other, and then myself. I had to go to the root of my problems and discover the generation bondage that plagued my family decades before I was born.

***

Even though my big brother, Trivet, and I were both raised together in foster care, we responded and processed our circumstances very differently. When I journeyed to discover our origin, he seemed to be at peace with the unknown. The unknown haunted me often at night as I laid wide-awake throughout my teenage and young adult years.

It was hard to believe I was divorced after two months of marriage, lost the support of my foster care family, and slept on Trivet's couch as a 24-year-old man. I fought tooth and nail to piece back together who I was. Through the grace of God, I discovered a voice I had shut off for decades. It took a total of six months to get back on my feet, thrive as a community leader and become a director of a community center in Buffalo, NY.

I prayed to find the source of my pain and misfortune as I encountered demons locked away that I tackled on. With little to no resources, I travelled to city courts, paid for sealed records, and went to former neighborhoods I used to live while searching for my family. All dead-end roads. My mother's first name was the vital piece of information that led me down the last chapter of this book, "The Hero's Rabbithole".

The trend in my life was isolation. I felt isolated as a child, teen, and an adult. Basketball became my outlet as a teen as I had used it to escape the pressures of life. It was only a temporary solution to a permanent problem, identity. The issues of life all stemmed from the question many of us wrestle with. "Who am I?"

***

I wrestled with many questions that wandered in my mind for years growing up without parents. Questions like, "What if the hope in which I am looking for does not come? "What if waiting for a miracle or significant event to motivate me does not happen? What do we do when there is nothing left to do?" Life responded to my question as the answers came to me at my lowest points. When all the noise was quiet, I was able to listen to the answers. Answers are usually simple, but as people we overcomplicate things. My inner courage awakened during several different occasions within my life and it left me with the answer to "Who am I?"

When I went away to college to play basketball, the isolation and seclusion ignited another side of me I was unfamiliar with. I discovered other gifts other than dribbling a basketball. I did not recognize the potential of the gift until my senior year of college one of my mentors, TRiO Student Support Services Director, approached me.

"Schwartzen, have you thought about the scholarship offer that TRIO SSS awards students who had shown much perseverance during their college studies? I think you should consider applying for it. What do you think?"

"Yeah, I know that scholarship," I said. "I've applied for it every year and never received it. There's no sense of applying for it now ya know?" My self-doubt used to get the best of me.

"Schwartz," the Director continued. "I think you tell people the comfortable version of your college journey. I heard you share your actual story at the university forum. You shared your truth. It was raw, unedited and authentic. You've attended this university for four years and it was the first time that any of the staff, faculty and students had ever heard about your personal experience. Your transition from inner-city New York to rural Upper Peninsula, Michigan as a struggling youth is unique. If you shared the story on the process in which you became this well-rounded leader we see today, I bet it would increase your likelihood of being selected as a Leadership Award Recipient. Show people the real you."

Their words rang through my ears like a firehouse bell. The inability to see my own value was a liability, but therefore mentors are important. They challenge our comfort zone. I agreed and it became the first time I wrote about being a foster child growing up in inner-city New York. I submitted my story; I was awarded the leadership award shortly after. My story was shared at the state capital, but it was only the beginning.

My story became known yet inconsistent from my fear of the truth. I did not know my biological family. With my birth records changed after being adopted as a teen, I spent decades putting pieces of my story together. Even though Trivet and I became well-rounded men, we struggled to keep foundation to solidify our growth. It was an uncomfortable situation that I did not accept. What I call, "unaccepted dilemma" I set out to conquer my biggest fear.

Our everyday heroes that go away to fight for freedom never return home the same way they left. It feels like something is missing, as if the peace of mind they had before the war was gone forever. Wars looks different for everyone, but ultimately the war begins and ends in the mind. The war I had been through was the war against poverty, ignorance, and mental illness.

I used to believe my childhood was designed to keep me from discovering who I was. The mix of mental and physical abuse can keep most from reaching their potential. What separates the good from the great is their ability to not only overcome challenges but the person they become after all is said and done. It is what separates Batman from Bane, Superman from Lex Luther, Spiderman from Shocker, and Profession X from Magneto. One difference separates the two, it's called choice. Gifts are used for good or evil, there is no middle ground.

Within the mentioned Superhero movies, I have realized that even a beaten down person with an ounce of hope can still ignite a movement. In 2011, Marvel released a movie called X-Man: First Class. The "mutants" were nearly killed off by the humans and Magento decided to become a supervillain while Professor X decided to hold onto hope believing the humans will someday see the good in "mutants." This is how I saw my life for a while. I will start at the beginning.

Chapter 1: Diversabilities

"Definitions belong to the definers, not the defined."

–Toni Morrison

Like most people, at one point I believed the reward for good grades in school results in a good college which led to a good paying job. A good paying job leads to having a good spouse, having great kids, then retirement. The American Dream, right? The life I lived was a much different narrative, certainly not the American Dream narrative. Being a young black boy with no mom or dad living in Brooklyn, NY painted a different reality. It was not until I reached adulthood where I discovered a way to change the given narrative of a foster child in an impoverished environment.

I became conscious of foster care when I was six years old. The word "abandoned" dwelled in my mind at that age. Some adults within foster care called us "abandoned" since that was the story I was told. My older brother Trivet, who I called "Pepe" growing up, we were always around each other. We wore matching outfits, shoes, and backpacks. Being the younger of the two orphaned boys, I did what I could to get out of his shadow and be my own person. Being young, energetic, full of excitement, and always smiling happy and I was known as the "cute wild child."

At six-years-old, we lived in a three-bedroom apartment where Pepe and I shared a bunk bed in Bronx, NY. The Bronx was our home for five years with my first foster mom, Cece. She *was* my mother. I was accepted for my behavior and Pepe was calmer and accepted for his behavior. Even though we were blood brothers, our behavior was on opposite ends of the spectrum.

It was rumored that Pepe and I were found in an apartment in Brooklyn, NY at one and two years old. We were taken into foster care when the neighbors called the police. New York City during the 70's, 80's and 90's was known for its heavy drug epidemic before the mayor cleaned up the city. Living in the South Bronx during the late 90's, I saw plenty of drug users and dealers. It is the harsh reality for children growing up in the inner-city. I always thought my birth mother was a drug user since it was common back then.

Cece had a son that helped raise us. I thought he was my father for a while. He always looked tough and we were the same skin complexion. He was the neighborhood "Ace" (A term known in urban New York referring to Ace Boogie, a boss in the streets of a movie called Paid in Full). He and I always spent time together as he always made me laugh from his jokes.

Most of my childhood, I embodied the narrative of children open, full of life and energy. Between social workers, teachers, counselors, other foster parents, it seemed like my playfulness was a disease as they always looked serious when I smiled. I often acted before I thought since my impulses got the best of me. I was very impressionable and naturally picked up on subtle cues and body language. I had a burning curiosity to learn about any and everything. I knew I had super strength since I was stronger than other kids. Most of all, I despise being told what to do. I learned lessons the hard way. Observing Pepe and other foster children shaped my perception on how I saw myself as different. Pepe rarely smiled and his demeanor was always reserved.

We had plenty of neighborhood friends in the Bronx. There was a neighborhood park where kids from the surrounding project buildings played. Even though we lived in the "ghettos" the people looked out for one another. Community members greeted each other, and I was carefree. At Cece's house, I felt loved. I hugged my Pitbull every day and was happy despite being a foster child. Some time passed before Cece decided to move out of the Bronx to a city called Allentown in Pennsylvania right before my seventh birthday.

Initially, I did not like the change, but quickly, Allentown, PA grew on me. I realized that I did not like the Bronx apartment as much as I thought I did since we lived in project housing. We moved into a four-story house with six bedrooms in a much cleaner neighborhood. The new house had a porch, a basement, a backyard, and a shed for our dog. Our room was much larger than the one in the Bronx.

We always had food, water, clothes, video games and action figures to play with. In Allentown, Pepe and I had some friends we called our "cousins" who lived up the street from us. We went over to their house on the weekends. Pepe, myself, our cousins and other neighborhood kids played games like cops and robbers, freeze tag, steal the bacon, and my personal favorite game manhunt. Manhunt was a game where the players hid from player that "hunted" everyone. The "hunter" had to discover where everyone else was hiding and it had to be in a specific range of the house. When the "hunter" caught the hunted, they had to help find the other player that hid. The game required creativity, and I was creative. Since I had a small body frame, I hid in places that most players could not get into. I often climbed trees, hid in trash cans and bushes until I got bored.

Aside of our cousins' house, Pepe and I attended the Boys and Girls Club of Allentown every day after school. At 7-years-old, it became my second home. It was kid paradise. It had an indoor pool, where I learned to swim, which was one of my favorite activities. My favorite area was the foosball table since I destroyed Pepe at foosball. The only thing that was better than destroying Pepe was teaming up with him and destroying other kids. We competed in races, games, and other club activities that I won nearly every time. I learned at an early age that I loved to compete.

Self-Esteem

Pepe and I attended the same school for one year in Allentown. I was one of those kids that did not like school. Instead, I was more interested in the action going on outside the building. Students organized themselves in racing competitions each morning before class started. Competition is where I was introduced to self-esteem.

The school building was on a slope, as soon as runners ran from the top of the hill, they picked up speed toward the bottom. They risked falling and hurting themselves, which several kids did. High risk, high reward. If you lost the race, the walk of shame back up the hill brought criticism and judgement. Like most children, the pressure of being accepted by peers called my name.

I envisioned myself winning the race every day until I decided to participate. I told myself *the only thing better than watching them run is to join in on the action*. The black and Hispanic students dominated the races but occasionally a white boy or girl won. After weeks of observing, I decided to compete. I had a burning desire inside of me that was ready to be unleashed.

The day of my first race, I felt confident. All eyes were on me since I was a new runner. The glares from 40+ spectators on the sidewalk attempted to discourage me, but my mind was locked in on the street road ahead. Focused, determined, and willing to give this race everything I had. I briefly glanced at my opponent to the left of me as I took my runner's stance. I turned my head to look down the sloped hill seeing myself winning.

I breathed deeply as my lungs filled with the coolness in the air. The wind blew a slight breeze as my heroic heartbeat increased the adrenaline being pumped into the chambers of my chest. Time stopped. The word "Go!" blasted through my eardrum like a shotgun. I took off down the street like "The Flash". Before I could consciously blink, the race was over. My first race was followed by a satisfying rush fueled by the feeling of winning. Adrenaline made me feel alive. I made it a habit to place my hand over my chest to feel my heart pounding as sweat dripped down from my forehead over my face. The competition increased my appetite to dominate the other runners.

After my first race, one of the students popped the question. "What's your name son?" It was my first time being recognized by my peers after appearing superior. At that time, I was used to others butchering my name. "Shorts, shorty, Arnold, sportsman, squashy, squatty…" and every other name except my own.

"Schwartzenegger," I told him, "My name is Schwartzenegger."

Quickly, I earned the reputation of the "fastest kid in school." I loved competing against older students; it was more challenging. Some called it cocky, but racing defined my self-worth, it brought me recognition. Most kids define their self-worth based on their academic performance, I based mine on my running performance. I was the hungry wolf on the top of the hill. By the time I was 8 years old, I discovered ego as my demeanor developed into that of "Mr. Big Shot." I attracted cute girls and of course I did my best to impress them. It was instinctive. Girls did not show me attention prior to winning races.

My brother Pepe was the exact opposite. Instead of racing, he focused on schoolwork. Majority of the reason I did not like school was the constant comparison to Pepe's academic standards. Teachers praised Pepe for his "brightness, smarts, and intelligence." Winning races did not impress teachers. Academics were a different kind of competition, where being fast on your feet did not make you superior. Pepe's ability to think faster than others set him apart from "academic mediocrity."

Teachers asked questions, students gave answers. Peers who answered questions first and correct were the star pupils. Pepe was one of those star pupils. Being a "star pupil's" younger brother, placed a disappointing standard on me. Pepe, along with other academic overachiever, were in the school section called

"Eagles." Academic achievers soared above the mediocre students. Teachers pressured me to be an "Eagle," like Pepe. I was not an eagle, I considered myself a lion. Lions dominate in their terrain on land. That's how I looked at myself. I was content with it. In the school halls, the environment was the sky. Lions could not dominate the sky, but eagles could.

We were opposites. Pepe was quiet, I was loud. He was taller, I was short. Pepe kept to himself while I was outspoken. We were both young black boys with the same upbringing yet had completely different personalities. We shared the same second grade teacher, who referred to Pepe as "the brightest student she had ever taught."

"Why can't you be like Pepe?" Those words brought early sibling rivalry.

It never crossed my mind, "*why couldn't I be like Pepe?*" Instead, I often questioned, "*why can't they see me for what I do well?*"

When Pepe transferred to a school for the gifted, his name left a legacy behind. Pepe's absence was more appreciated than my presence. My name got me in trouble at school as I wrote my full name, "Schwartzenegger," on my name tag in the third grade. Writing my full name resulted in a phone call home. Apparently, the teacher thought I wrote the wrong name.

Cece had a black southern parental style of raising her kid. "The teacher is always right." Phone calls home were not tolerated. Neither were fairy tales or fantasies. She did not have us believe in Santa Claus or the Tooth Fairy (Sorry if I spoiled it for you), but she loved to buy us things. The final Christmas we spent together, Cece bought Pepe and I skateboards, skates, scooters and my all-time favorite Christmas gift, new bikes.

I loved bikes and never expected to have my own. I used to get in trouble for stealing bikes around the neighborhood. The day I got my new bike I took it outside, hopped and went flying down the road.

Cece shouted "Go, Schwartz Go!" The world I knew was behind me from the exhilaration. When I reached the end of the block, I noticed Pepe was not behind me. He was nowhere in sight. I rode my bike back to the house. He was on his bike, crying. He was unable to keep his balance on his new bike. At that moment, I took notice of the pattern in his inability to be physically competent like me.

***

Cece's oldest daughter brought Pepe and I to the skating rink to use our new skates. I fell in love with the place. She brought us every weekend as it was the highlight of my week. At the rink, I never thought about living up to my big brother's academic standards since I did what I loved. Skating brought me to a place where I felt above the pressures of life. I loved showing out on the skating rink especially against Pepe. *As long as I continued to skate there was not a single thing that could stop me from enjoying life.* Shortly after, life threw me an unanticipated obstacle.

Chapter 2: Upside Down Worldview

As an eight-year-old, I was secure in my physical abilities but accepted my weaknesses in academics. Cece noticed I was active and placed me in karate class and dance practice where I performed on stage to showcase my gifts. My view on life was healthy. All was well but little did I know that life can be unpredictable even as a child.

In the Marvel movie Spider-Man 2 (2003), Tobey Maguire who plays Peter Parker, began to lose his superpowers. Peter decided to visit the doctor. Physically, he was ok, but the doctor suggested it there might be something wrong in his mind. After briefing the doctor about a dream "his friend" had, the doctor asked questions.

"So, what does 'Spider-Man' think of himself?"

Peter answers, "that's the thing doc, he doesn't know what to think of himself."

The doctor responds, "Nothing is worse than uncertainty, maybe you're not supposed to be the person climbing up a wall, which is why 'Spider-Man' keeps falling. You always have a choice, Peter."

After the conversation, Peter Parker made the choice to no longer be Spider-Man. There are times in life where people make the choice to stop operating in their God given gift. When others chose to no longer use their abilities, it is the world around them that suffers more than the actual person.

"When one chooses not to use their gift, it is not you who suffers, but the world around you."

-Schwartzen Precil

In March 2003, my life changed forever as I was unable to use my physical abilities. When I could not do what I loved, I felt like a wanderer. I lost myself. My identity was molded based on what I did well. Even though my superpowers did not enable me to climb walls or spin webs, my confidence made me feel invincible. The pain from the mental grief people go through when confidence is lost is a pain the human spirit is not meant to bare.

The day I lost my abilities I ran through the halls at the Boys and Girls Club. I was given the "take it outside" look so I decided to play tag with another kid, and I ran down the stairs outside the clubhouse. *I left them way behind me*, I thought to myself. I turned around and the kid was within arm's reach behind me running full speed. Instinctively, I ran onto the sidewalk and into the street while it was pitch black outside.

I did not see any cars in the street. Unfortunately, one car had its headlights shut off driving down the block. In a split second, the impact from the car left my shoes on the ground as my body catapulted in the air. The car never stopped. A hit and run. I blacked out. I woke up lying on my back. I did only what an 8-year-old can do at that moment.

"AHHHH!" I gave a loud yell.

My right leg was numbed by the pain. The ambulance arrived within minutes. I was placed on the stretcher as my eyes met the sea of people on the sidewalk. I saw kids crying and clenching their fists in anger. I was the center of attention. I noticed Pepe's eyes were wide open as he looked at me in disbelief. the ambulance. *What just happened?* I thought.

I laid in the hospital bed after they took x-rays. There were no serious injuries or a need for surgery. I was given crutches and Cece picked me up and we left the hospital. My night was far from over. I went to sleep in pain in my right leg. From that point on, all I could hear were criticisms from peers, friends, and family as their words floated through my conscience. This was my introduction to Fear as I heard its voice. *I was a mess and I deserved to be hit by that car.* It was my first time being defined by a mistake but certainly not my last. It was the start to the end of my childhood.

The questions about my hurt leg was background music to the negative thoughts dancing between my ears. After a week, I tossed the crutches in the trash and walked with a limp leg. It was painful to walk, but the embarrassment and shame the crutches brought stung a little more. The routine walks home became burdensome.

My superpowers were taken away as the world around me shifted. I noticed others hid their negative facial expressions around me. I felt embarrassed to go to school, so I skipped the Boys and Girls Club for a few days to be by myself. The days were long, the nights were longer. Discouragement led to depression as I felt lonelier by the day. Life moved on without me. I no longer coped with the comparisons to Pepe or the negative words that drowned my childish mind.

***

Two weeks after the accident, a rush of enthusiasm led me to run at school. I attempted to run full speed, but a sharp pain devoured my leg. Unable to finish, I grabbed my book bag and took the walk of shame into the school building. I returned to the Boys and Girls Club to get my mind off the humiliation I brought to myself.

My physical abilities were imprisoned by my body. The desire to be physically active did not subside. The flurry of emotions erupted as I experienced both anger and angry sadness. Unable to process my unhealthy state of mind, I blamed the Boys and Girls club for my accident. I thought *maybe skating would help ease the pain.* When I returned to the roller rink Cece's daughter pulled me aside.

"Schwartzenegger, mom told me about the car accident. I want you to take it easy when you're skating today ok?"

"Okay," I responded while secretly planning to skate off the built-up tension.

When we arrived, I put my skates on my feet and went cruising down the hardwood. At least, that's how I imagined it went. My right leg was completely uncooperative. My legs were unable to move swiftly. I was rusty yet still happy to be at the rink. Reality kicked in the moment Pepe zoomed by me on his skates. I was puzzled. *Had the accident messed up my leg to the point that I couldn't skate fast anymore?*

I pushed my legs as hard as possible to catch Pepe. When he saw me coming, he left me to eat his dust. In a matter of two weeks, Pepe was a better skater than me. It was salt to an open wound. I was powerless without my physical abilities. It was the earliest depressing moment I can recall. The desire to skate left as my heart sank down to my butt. I cried during the car ride home as Cece's daughter held me in her arms. *How did a car accident take away so much in a matter of weeks? I can't do anything right.* The negative thoughts swarmed me as my life no longer made sense.

Determined Spirit

My body had betrayed me. I was a victim of life's cruel joke. The last resort was to ride my bike. My bike was in the basement which had a flight of twelve stairs separating the upstairs and the downstairs. My bike weighed nearly 50lbs and was nearly three feet tall. I placed my helmet on top of my head and pushed up on the handlebars to move the bike up one stair at a time.

As I pushed the bike, my clothes began to stick to me from the accumulation of sweat. The bike weighed as much as an elephant. *What did I get myself into?* I looked over my right shoulder down the stairs wondering if I should let the bike roll back down. If I let the bike go, I risked the possibility of letting roll on top of me and being stuck. I looked ahead; I was more than halfway up the stairs. *I might as well get it up there and try to enjoy a nice bike ride.* Exhausted, I debated if the reward from riding the bike outweighed the pain of pushing the bike up the final stairs.

Fear yelled *STOP! Will letting the bike go hurt you as much as the pain from the car accident? Probably not.*

It was followed up by a small voice I called 'Truth' which whispered. *What good will it bring to you if you allow the bike to roll back downstairs? Keep going. You love to ride the bike, so ride it.*

I listened to the whisper and pushed with every ounce of strength I had. Pushing the bike to the top of the stairs seemed unlikely, but it was possible. Each stair stepped up on became harder than the last stair. I exhausted all my energy and I had the final three steps to climb up. Physically, the bike was too heavy, and my head hurt. Mentally, the internal conversation I had with myself left me drained and confused.

I began to loosen my grip on the handlebar to allow the bike roll down the stairs. Then, an image popped into my head. I imagined what *I* looked like in the moment. Sweating with my hands tightly gripped to the yellow Mongoose handlebars. I nearly let go until a burst of unfamiliar energy took control of my body. It pushed my physical limitations. This unfamiliar internal strong-willed voice gave a loud cry. "AAAHHHH!" Up the step it went with one final push.

I breathed heavily as I slobbered in sweat. An ugly sight. With one final push, I got the bike to the top of the stairs and gasped for air. An improbable victory, but a victory, nonetheless. By the time I got the bike outside I was too tired to ride it. Still, I hopped on the bike, went up and down the block a few times with no pain in my right leg. This was the first time I saw an obstacle make way for an unforeseen opportunity.

"You're already hurt, you're already in pain

get a reward from it!"

-Dr. Eric Douglas Thomas

In the Marvel movie, "Black Panther," there is a scene fight scene between King T'Challa aka the Black Panther (played by Chadwick Bosman) and King M'Baku leader of the Jabari Tribe. During the fight, King T'Challa is without his Black Panther strength and showed signs of losing the fight. M'Baku bear hugs the King T'Challa and head butts him three times. It looks like the T'Challa will lose the fight. The nation of Wakanda gasps at his tight situation.

"No powers! No claws! No special suit! Just a boy. NOT FIT TO LEAD!" M'Baku mocks.

As the disillusioned T'Challa attempted to regain consciousness, he hears an echoey voice. "Show him who you are!" The voice (from his mother) propelled him to gain internal strength where he reaffirms himself out loud by reminded himself of who he is.

That one scene displays hidden potential within individuals who do not need their superpower to overcome obstacles. Sometimes in moments of defeat, the spirit of determination shows up at the right time. We are given obstacles to elevate us from our current situation.

In the face of opposition, we are given two choices; One is a way that will show you how to overcome doubt and despair, which I call "Fear." The other choice is to listen to the Fear and feel defeated. At 8-years-old, I had willpower of a true warrior. Unfortunately, I could not see it at that age. My low self-esteem kept me from seeing the beauty within myself. Later, I became motivated in situations of my extreme discomfort. I was a glimpse of my courageous spirit.

"Comparison is a sure way to kill confidence."

-Schwartzen Precil

Days passed as my heart grew bitter from my physical inabilities. My mind drifted to focus on the negative. I watched as Pepe used his abilities to play the violin. My inadequacy reminded me to feel neglected. My life felt loveless as I reminded myself that Cece was only my foster mom. *Where is my real mom?*

***

I was in my own head at the Boys and Girls club the following week, as I attempted to take Pepe's Gameboy from out of his hands. His hands tightly gripped the Gameboy. It was a war of will. I became enraged and screamed. The staff broke us apart and placed us in an office. The main staff was shocked to see us brothers fighting. We sat in an all-white room with a brown office desk and a couple of chairs. The door was shut as we were questioned about the incident. My face showed it all, I was pissed. I could not think clearly. My anger became the elephant in the room. Pepe kept calm as usual.

"How's the leg treating you Schwartzen?" The staff asked.

"Fine," clearly showing an attitude.

The staff directed questions to Pepe about why we fought. They talked as if I was not in the room. I was infuriated with the lack of attention as it triggered the feeling of inadequacy. I spoke.

"No! That's not what happened." My voice commanded attention. My eyes burned a hole in the ground as unfiltered words sprung off my tongue. We drifted off the topic off the Gameboy and into questions about our life in foster care.

The questions continued as I had to prove to the adult I knew as much as my big brother. I showed I could speak up for myself as Pepe stayed quiet. My words had value as her facial expression and her pen followed my words. Words rolled off my tongue and onto paper. I felt important and recognized. It was refreshing to get my thoughts out of my head. Unaware of the words I spoke my words contributed to the change in trajectory in our lives.

Several days later, two adults pulled me out of class and escorted me to a white van where I met Pepe with several pieces of luggage.. The white van drove to the foster care agency office in Manhattan, NY. We stayed in a colorful room playing with toys until a tall Haitian man with a gold tooth attempted to claim us. He was said to be our uncle or a relative. We were unable to stay with him I was unaware of what was taking place.

The world had revealed it true colors, it was cruel to those who expressed themselves freely. Foster care disregarded any feelings children might have had. I desired to go back to Cece's house. Pepe and I went to a couple of other foster houses before finally being placed at a household in Staten Island, NY, the forgotten borough.

***

The hours spent on the road in the white van gave me time to think. I stared out the window during the van ride wondering *when I was going to see my mommy again. I'm sure it was only a matter of time.* I attempted to stay positive as we approached the door of the stranger's home. The neighborhood was clean as the sun shined on the beige door and golden doorknob. With luggage in one hand and anticipation in the other, the social worker knocked on the beige door.

Why am I here? How long am I staying? I imagined myself fighting and eating bad food at the group home since I overheard the social worker talk on the phone. I imagined a war zone. Turned out to be our final foster home. The friendly greetings of a tall black man who wore a big smile, no front teeth, with a bald head caught me by surprise.

"HEY!" He spoke with the enthusiasm of a used car salesman. "Come on in!" My eyes planted on his four missing teeth from both top and bottom rows. We walked in the house and I noticed the beige colored carpet matched the couch set in the living room. There was an upstairs part of the house like Cece's house, but this house did not have a backyard, a shed, my dog, or a basement. *Where's my mommy?* I thought.

We were introduced to four foster kids living in the house, three of which were siblings. They were lined up shoulder to shoulder ready to meet us. The four foster children in the house were within the same age range. Abdul was the youngest of the siblings, he and I were the same age. Aeisha was the only girl of the three siblings, her and Pepe were the same age. The oldest of the three was JD, who was the tallest child, looked meaner and very different than his siblings.

We were ordered to go upstairs to our new room. Four boys in 8' x 8' room was uncomfortable, but we had no choice. Pepe and I took the top bunks then reported downstairs to have a talk with the man with no teeth. He introduced his wife and himself as they told us to call them "Mr. Les" and his wife "Ms. I." His wife was a heavy-set woman whose eyes were glued to the TV. Her hands moved to the rhythm of her soft voice every time she spoke. She wore fancy jewelry that often-made noise.

"In this house we abide by my rules. We don't welcome questions or opinions. You two are guests here you understand me?" The man with no teeth reiterated that we were only there for a short stay. Being who I was, I quickly forgot his words and reaped the consequences during mealtime.

***

A loud, "come eat!" travelled all the way to our rooms from the lower floor. Yelling in the house was a norm. We were each given one peanut butter and jelly sandwich for lunch. One sandwich left me very hungry and decided to ask the man with no teeth for another sandwich.

"This ain't ya other house boy, only one sandwich per child. Didn't I say no questions?" *What just happened?* I tried to process his response, but his intimidating look shut down any words I might have spat back. *At Cece's house, I had two peanut butter and jelly sandwiches for lunch. Why do I only get one at this house? At Cece's house I made my own lunch, I knew how to slap some spread between bread and eat it.* I kept my thoughts to myself. The mean mug he gave me was followed by dirty looks from the other foster children.

I struggled adjusting to the new rules of the foster home. My entire routine had changed. I used to take medication at Cece's house by a certain time, but at this new house I did not have any medication. The medications kept my thoughts at bay, and they helped me sleep. Without them my mind developed survival mechanisms very quickly. I thought to myself. *I gotta do what needs to be done in order to survive in this place. These people don't care if I starve.* The man with no teeth gave me what I called the "death glare." It was his way of asserting dominance through nonverbal communication.

I laid in bed wide awake for hours on end as my eyes glued to the ceiling only four inches above my face. This happened for weeks as the bed I slept in was all but comfortable. My body did not correspond with the early bedtime hours. My hungry belly often kept me up at night. Dinner portions were as small as lunch portions. It was poverty. For weeks, I climbed off the top of the bunk bed in the middle of the night to steal food. Some nights I stole from the fridge, other nights I only ate snacks. I entered the kitchen as darkness surrounded me in the middle of the night. *So much for the man with no teeth denying me food.*

Some nights I pretended to be asleep when I was wide awake. Other nights, the man with no teeth entered the room. He stood in the middle of the room for about ten seconds, walked out and slammed the door behind him. I found it very bizarre. Then again, my whole world was upside down. I pondered through the mysterious thoughts as a child. *How long will I be here? Is everything that I knew and loved really gone?* I did my chores, at my food and went to bed at 7:30pm, two hours earlier than when I went to bed at Cece's house. Pepe seemed content as his face remained expressionless.

Chapter 3: Divide and Conquer

"You can't separate peace from freedom because no one can be at peace unless they have their freedom."

-Malcolm X

It did not take long for the man with no teeth to turn Pepe, myself, and the other foster children against each other. They drilled us all with questions for hours until we were mentally exhausted. We were manipulated into giving them Cece's number. When Pepe told the story about how we were taken out of Cece's house, I interrupted.

"No that's not what happened." I spoke concisely. My voice penetrated the closed minds in the room as their eyes locked on mine. Pepe and I went back and forth about why we were taken from the other foster home. Our broken bond was exploited as our sibling rivalry took a turn for the worse. They spoke on the phone with our former foster parents.

"Oh, so you were joining gangs when you were at that woman's house?" They spoke.

"No," I responded in disbelief.

"Seemed like you ruined Pepe's life Schwartzen since he was in the school for the gifted. You're a damn thief, and you led a gang at school."

War had begun. No time was lost as I was labelled a delinquent and other condescending names. I could not hide my anger as my blood boiled and I clenched my fist as tears strolled down my cheeks.

SMACK! The man with no teeth struck me in the face. My 65lb body hit the floor hard. His heavy hand left a huge red mark across my face.

"You mad? I know you not crying boy!" He pushed my hand away from my cheek as I rubbed the red spot.

"In this house, men don't cry, ya hear me!?"

I desperately erupted in tears as my voice cracked. I played right into his strategic plan to divide and conquer us foster children. The look of disgust wiped away any positive thoughts I might have had. Fear had manifested itself as my days of living in hell had just begun. My emotions could not be controlled as I was unable to keep my face and body from hiding the inner turmoil. Being slapped and punched for any facial expressions made me think on my toes. Pepe found favor in the eyes of the foster parent as he remained emotionless. His poker face was elite. I was in this by myself. *All this happened because I was hit by a car?* Fear dominated my thought process.

The man with no teeth called twice a day me to remind me of what I was. "Say 'I'm stupid. Say I'm a moron. Say I'm an idiot." When I refused, a slap in the face was followed. It was a lose-lose situation. The negative self-talk was embedded in my subconscious. Negative self-talk became their weapon of choice to oppress my creative young mind. His eyes told a cruel story life. Control. My insubordination was a liability to his control.

"You ruined Pepe's life once, don't do it again. Don't tell anybody anything that goes on in this house. Don't nobody want to be dragged along down with your mess!" *I was blamed for dragging Pepe's life through the mud.* Fear ignited as truth remained silent.

They spoke to Pepe often as if I was not in the room.

"Do not allow your brother bring you down the mud. Your life is good here, Schwartzen will end up in jail, he is a criminal. Do not go with him. He will soon go to another foster care house. You're allowed to stay here and live with us." They brainwashed Pepe to believe their house was one of the better homes in the foster care system. They convinced us both that my life was subjected to imprisonment. Attempting to speak up for myself was a hefty price to pay. I learned to keep my thoughts to myself. Whatever gifts I believed I possessed became that of a curse.

"...soon it will be the conquerors and the conquered. I would rather be the former."

-W'Kabi, Marvel's Black Panther

***

The days, months and years passed by. From sunup to sundown they it became second nature to walk around the house on eggshells. Every day was like the last except they reaped a different consequence. We submitted to the unspoken rules. Seeds of discord poured out of the walls as the hierarchical divide created a highly anxious environment. We were given one activity during the weekdays, watch TV.

I hated watching TV. It made my eyes hurt and I could not sit still. Anything beyond watching TV was forbidden. From playing outside, to having friends, and video games were only used on weekends. Being on the computer was forbidden and I felt like a fugitive. *Why were they isolating us? Could someone be out there looking for me as I am trapped here?* One thing was for sure, the freedom I had at Cece's house became a distant memory.

In 2019, most kids receive a smartphone between the ages of 10 and 12. By age 12, 50% of 12-year old's in America have a social media accounts and own a smartphone. Unlike today's world, the children of that household did not own before the age of 12, and when Pepe received his first phone at 13 years old, it was a flip phone. There was no luxury of browsing the Internet or texting a friend to talk as an outlet. We all endured the pain, some worse than others.

***

The foster parents forced JD to supervise us when they when out shopping, went on trips, or went on vacation. He was extremely controlling. From the TV, to the music, to the amount of air that circulated through the window. When JD did not get his way, his anger made him destructive. If we sneezed, coughed or laughed too loud he exploded. JD did what he wanted with no hesitation. When he wanted to leave the house, he left. He was the first kid to take his freedom by force when he was a teenager. His rebellion and immaturity were disregarded from the man with no teeth.

JD being the oldest, he had the most influence. JD modelled himself after gangsta rappers. From day one, he showed signs of severe mental illness. Many fights broke out, but JD rarely ever got in trouble. His allegiance to with the foster parents made him invincible. Snitching only made matters worse. We adopted the "street code" in the boy's room. The environment was a war zone. It was better to endure JD's bullying or fight rather than snitch on him. JD was and aspiring kingpin. His love for hood movies forced me to see the perpetrated negative images of a black man as a killer, drug dealer, or rapper. The media was clear as to what my future looked like as a young black male. The young black male had one of two options, in prison or dead by 21 years old.

Quickly, I realized the correlation between the foster house and prison. I observed the prison environment from TV. Both the spoken and unspoken rules between inmates and prison officials were just like the foster house. Prisons had a warden, guards, a facility, cells for inmates, and three meals a day. The unspoken rules among the prisoners were based on respect and relationships. Loyalty was a rare commodity. I learned to "trust no one, not even family." Prison was about getting money and laying low. That is what JD did, this is the principle I adapted.

Prisoners fought, stole, lied, and whatever else to survive. My survival skills were cultivated from years of having "hood" habits. Four black boys in a room with gangsta rap, bunk beds (prison cells), and egos? I had to survive. Our fights left bruises and broken furniture within the war zone. Between the ages of 8 and 13, I survived at any cost and carried that mentality until my third year of college.

"By any means necessary..."

-Malcolm X

Systemic Control

The man with no teeth became known as "the warden." Hood movies showed how wardens have a discreet relationship with one or several of the inmates to maintain control. JD was the warden's inside man among us prisoners since he was free from the warden's wrath. The warden did nothing to prevent JD from beating us up. The warden gave JD money occasionally. I interpreted it as the warden rewarding JD's obedience to maintain order.

Some of the warden's tactics of control included sending me to bed without food when I angered him. In his prison house, permission needed to be granted for bathing. I often walked around the house smelly. I only bathed once a week and our baths were limited to 10 minutes. He shouted, "This is a dictatorship!" as he sat in his chair watching his prized 72-inch TV. I interpreted his dictator leadership style to prepare us young black boys for prison in our future years. The prison rules were the norm for my rational thoughts. My emotions were numb

from the inability to express myself. This affected me as a
teenager as it was hard to show true affection.

The warden never cried, laughed, and or smiled. The
"death glare" he gave me was like a personal vendetta. I did not
let him see my cry. One time I cried as we watched the movie
"Set It Off." The warden stopped the movie and called me a
"sissy" for crying as a boy. He slapped me and sent me to bed
without food.

He said, "real men don't cry boy, wipe those tears
away!" The other foster kids laughed, as I could not help myself
from crying. I had to learn the art of the poker face that Pepe had
perfected.

*"It was better to hide built up emotions than be criticized for
expressing them."*

−Schwartzen Precil

The wife's role in the warden's house was very passive.
We had little to no interaction. She had plenty of opinion as we
lived under the same roof, but her presence was unfelt. The
warden and his wife argued often. Their verbal attacks on one
another was a norm to my dysfunction.

I tried to escape to Aeisha's room. Her room was
comforting as the light from the sun danced through the curtains.
We often watched shows together, sang songs and formed a
small bond. She had an array of struggles in the house as a young
black girl. She was not raised to love herself. Just like me, she
was taught to hate herself. If I was the black sheep, she was one
too. The amount of physical and emotional pain she endured
made me believe she was not going to make it to 18. Even with
the bond we shared, there was no loyalty as fear was still the
motivation to survive by any means.

The other foster kids snitched me out when I did things
wrong in order to stay on the warden's good side. I was always
given an unfair trial during "family meetings" With their word

against mine, I was always found guilty. There is power in numbers. If two people say a lie, and stick to that lie, it does not matter if that one person told the truth, two voices were always greater than one. Favor went to the majority, even if the majority was wrong.

I often made up scenarios since "I don't know" was an insufficient answer. Creating a false narrative was easier than telling the truth or since the words of "lying children" fell on deaf ears. There was no individuality since the collective voice overpowered the lone wolf. I was unsure of the expectations from my guardians. I could not look for help because it never arrived. I was persecuted for speaking my truth.

Accepting unacceptance

As my stock value dropped, Pepe's stock value progressed. The foster parents showered him with compliments speaking life over his future. "When you become a doctor, do not forget to bail Schwartzen out of jail." My depression began to knock down the walls of my willpower. My opportunity to speak my truth was presented when childcare services offered a therapy session for Pepe and me. I could no longer bare the depression within. Suicidal thoughts floated around my mind. Moments before we left to go to therapy the warden spoke.

"Don't you say a damn word that goes on in this house, you hear me?" Ignoring his words, I spoke as my heart desired to the psychiatrist. The warden, his wife and Pepe were in the room as I answered all the friendly lady's questions. Pepe did not do much talking as usual. After we returned to the house I was whooped for "saying too much."

They were beyond upset, and the psychiatrist could not save me. I shut down as my loveless heart grew cold. The foster parent's beliefs finally penetrated my subconscious mind. Their booming voices every day in the house slowly crept up as my voice of reason. All possessions were taken away, "even the clothes on my back that Cece bought, was mine," he stated.

The warden gave me nicknames like "snake, liar, thief, and JD number 2." The nicknames made me feel like a foreigner in my own skin. No creative expressions, no possessions, no chance to think for myself. It took only a few years but the freedom over my own body left as well. My reality worsened as I witnessed Aeisha get stomped beat and spat on in the household. She was labelled "delusional," for her attempting to speak up for herself. Her words did more harm than good. JD's ensured to keep her quiet from the secret he hid. Aeisha was my ray of hope if I was to speak my truth. His oppression worked and we kept our voices silent as we both suffered through his big secret.

***

As a preteen, the warden had placed me on a flight of stairs I called "the pit." When I sat in the pit, he forbade anyone to talk to me. "Act like he does not exist." For years, I lived as the nonexistent hole in the wall. I thought of it all as a bad dream. For two straight years, no one acknowledged me as I sat in solitary confinement. Did I mention the warden only had sight in one eye? Literally, he wore an eye patch sometimes. It prevented him from seeing the entire picture. I needed guidance, not solitary confinement. The more I sat on those stairs, the more out of place I felt, yet I embraced it. I showed all the signs of being a lost child screaming to be found, somewhere, somehow by someone. *Was anyone out there looking for me?*

***

As life moved on without me, I stayed out of the way in school. We were forbidden to tell anyone we were in foster care, especially in school. I did not have many friends in elementary school. I stayed to myself. One kid named A-Will was friendly to me in the third grade. He was kind enough to introduce himself to me as we stood in the dismissal line. A-Will was a lighter skin black boy, like me, except he had curly hair and was chubby for his age. He cracked jokes about some random TV shows that made me laugh. It was my first memory of laughter since arriving in Staten Island.

One time, a classmate skipped in front of A-Will and I while we were waiting in line. I did not think much of it until A-Will told the kid what he did was wrong. The confrontation escalated quickly as A-Will swung at the kid. A-Will beat the kid up right in front of me. I froze as I watched A-Will's face turn red after the teacher broke them apart. The teacher escorted A-Will out of the classroom and I did not see him again until high school. He became one of my closest friends as he embodied the heart of a hero. That memory represented justice and planted seeds of a fighting spirit. Even though his method was extreme, he stood up for himself. A-Will being who he had allowed me to think I can save myself one day.

***

Heart of a Hustla

Hustlas get what they get because they take by any means. I had a natural tendency to hustle. I hustled kids for their playing cards during elementary school not caring who I hurt in the process. As I hustled, Pepe was a choir boy singing and dancing in school performances. I admired yet envied his singing. The next year I joined the school choir but could not match the standard of excellence Pepe set. My self-esteem was too low. Being a choir member was not "cool" and I shied away from being myself. My home life had already tarnished my self-image. Even at school I was mentally imprisoner.

***

I spent time in the courtyard in elementary engaging in physical activities. I dominated in sports during recess as I loved to compete. Girls who were competitive caught my eye often. One girl made me so nervous my body froze when we made eye contact. She blew my mind by how well she played sports. Her skill set was more advanced than all the guys. Her level of fierceness was unmatched. Her long brown hair flowed naturally as she often wore a ponytail. Somehow, I found an ounce of courage to ask her to be my girlfriend. She became the chance to have something good for myself. Her basketball skills showed us guys that she was a real champion. I risked getting whooped by the warden to hear her voice when I snuck to use the phone to call her at night.

It was hard to believe she liked me how I liked her. *The world around me did not like me, how could she like me?* I did not like myself. We had been dating for months and did not share a single kiss. Fear convinced me she was not into me even though she was.

I began to question things. *Why was I not as courageous as I used to be?* I attempted to reflect on my years before I moved to Staten Island. Fear had already planted a full nest as it orchestrated my inability to believe to believe in myself. I hesitated to answer questions in school and my sense of courage slowly faded. Towards the end of 5th grade, I met someone who appeared to be a real-life superhero.

Image of hope

A tall white man walked into the cafeteria one day to see his wife, Mrs. Atlas, who was a kitchen staff. I was away from all the students at the time out corner. The tall white man was her husband. The tall white man took a seat right next to me in the time out corner about an arm's length from where I sat. He was middle aged; medium built and had droopy eyes. Less than two minutes later, a student with a pencil and paper in their hand walked up to the man.

"Can I have your autograph?" The student asked.

The student was asked to return to their seat by the kitchen staff. In the blink of an eye, the cafeteria full of students ran up to where the tall white man and I sat. All the excitement and commotion piqued my curiosity. *Who is this guy? What does he do?* I watched in disbelief how someone could attract that much excitement from others. *He had to be a superhero*, I thought. He looked at me then gave an inviting smile as he gestured for me to sit closer to him

My mind replayed the kids rushing towards him as the tall white man asked me a question. I came to my senses and we spoke about the World Wrestling Confederation (WWF). I watched WWF on a weekly basis as I told him whom I liked watching the most. As the conversation moved on, the celebrity image that I had about this popular man faded. He was human. Capable of mistakes, as he mentioned a few of his own. *So, he makes mistakes too?* He shared encouraging words.

"Even the most popular people have their battles Schwartzen. You and I are no different."

To end the conversation, he asked me, "Who's your favorite wrestler in the WWF?"

"The Rock."

"My wife says you're up here away from the other kids too often. I tell you what, if Mrs. Atlas tells me that you haven't gotten in trouble at lunch for an entire week then I'll get you 'The Rock' action figure. We got a deal?"

Teddy Atlas reaching out for a handshake was the first time an adult treated me with an ounce of respect as a child. Sure, of myself I shook his hand, "deal."

He stood up, walked toward the exit, and left through the back doors. When lunch was dismissed, all the kids ran up to me and asked me "what was it like talking to 'The Teddy Atlas,'" saying "you're so lucky", and "my dad loves that guy" etc.

He was a man of his word. Mrs. Atlas gave me the action figure two weeks later. I needed someone to believe in me, if even for a moment. At ten-years-old, I did not believe I could do good, but Teddy Atlas challenged me. Out of the dozens of students who wanted to see Teddy Atlas up close, he chose to speak to me. I proved that I could reach a goal I set for myself. A hero who did not wear a cape gave that chance to me. It sparked some hope in me.

***

My best friend in the fifth grade was from Nigeria. He went to church and often told me about messages he received the previous Sunday.

"We're all brother's and sister's in God's eyes," he used to tell me. I did not consider the people I lived with family, which was okay since I had Manny.

On the final ride home from the elementary school bus, Manny and I said our goodbyes. He told me "he loved me like a brother." Manny saw the good in me, even though I thought I was a bad person. Moments before I hopped off the bus, he gave me a hug. I held back my tears since it was forbidden for me to cry. I had not heard the words "I love you" in so long. It was refreshing. He said it was the presence of "God" that made me feel like that. I told him I loved him too. I went back into the foster home to be reminded that there was no God because the hell I lived in only worsened throughout middle school.

Chapter 4: Forming a Supervillain

The environment that surrounds children plays a significant role during my stages of puberty. As my mind developed, more questions formed. My world was full of confusion. I coped by joining a street gang from a local neighborhood. The street influence made me the worst version of myself. Eventually, I started my own crew in middle school in attempts to be a kingpin.

We were sent to summer school for several years in one of the roughest neighborhoods in Staten Island. My survival skills enhanced quickly being in a rough neighborhood. My sixth sense developed as it kept me from dangerous situations. In the hood, hopelessness was sold was on every corner in the form of poison. Most people knew life through the lens of poverty. A blind eye was turned to those who were prisoners to their own mind.

I formed my own reality as I lived through the pain. My homies from the streets called me "SDot" as the name Schwartzenegger was nearly buried alive. I formed a "super ego" from the built-up pressure spending years in silence. By middle school, the negative and suicidal thoughts were stronger than ever. No one was not coming to save me. No one was coming to save me.

***

A personal favorite superhero movie is the Dark Knight Rises starring Christian Bale as Batman. At the climax of the Dark Knight Rises, Batman attempted to escape from a hole called "the pit." Attempt after attempt he failed, until a wise man gave him personal insight that he used to escape from "the pit." It is not *what* he does to get out of "the pit" but *how* he does it. Bane, being the supervillain, came out of that same hole when he was a child. When he escaped, he knew he had a plan to give the world a taste of its own medicine.

I also enjoyed reading Marvel's X-Men series with the super villain Magneto. With his indwelling anger awakened by his childhood trauma. It fueled his superhuman abilities as his family was taken away from him at an early age. Displaying destructive behavior as a child, made me see myself within Magneto. I too allowed my anger to control me during my middle school years.

In a poverty-stricken foster home, summer camp was nothing like my experience I had in Pennsylvania. Summer camp in Staten Island was less of a camp and more of a survival of the fittest boot camp. The number of drugs sold and used in the neighborhood was unbelievable. Staff and campers fought frequently. You were either tough or you were not. There was no in-between. The jungle exposed those who were motivated by fear. In that neighborhood, I wore a hardened exterior posture as a mask until it became second nature.

Campers smelled weakness like a pack of hyenas after prey. We were treated like animals, some of us acted as though we were. I considered myself a lion from my bold actions to do things most kids were afraid to do. Pepe was an eagle as his mind attempted to stay afloat above the poverty around him. The other foster kids were gorillas, and West Brighton was the jungle. My survival skills were put to the test in the streets for years. I adapted the "keep to yourself attitude." The words that left your mouth came at a high cost as gang members were very territorial. This is where living with a gangbanger was a benefit.

None of us foster kids were bothered since JD had juice in the streets.

The summer school we attended was built like a corrections facility. Medal bars on the classroom windows with security guards at every entrance. The first day of summer school there were eight kids in my class. All young black boys. I kept quiet and observed the other kids. The lights were off, and the classroom desks were tagged with graffiti gang symbols. The students looked as if they were at war as the scars on their arms and necks with missing teeth told stories of pain. The teacher took attendance just before two students began arguing.

One of the boys lost his temper and charged at the other. The two boys went pound for pound. The teacher stayed clear from the fight as a kid grabbed a broom from the corner to swing like a baseball bat. He swung it as the teacher attempted to grab it but was instead hit. She ran out of the classroom to call security.

My eyes captured the moments as the two boys were out for blood. My heart tapped danced on my tongue as Fear crawled up my spine. Only a heartbeat away from crying, I witnessed the black on black crime propaganda in performance only six inches in front of. Paranoia kicked in as I felt the attack on me next. My peripheral glued to the other black boys smirking as they sat back spectating.

As security barged in the room, I looked outside the window through the metal bars only to meet the reality of being caged in. Window padded bars in a classroom. What reality was being created for me? *This is prison,* Fear said. There was no possibility of jumping out of the window and escaping to freedom. Window padded bars separated me from the freedom I thirsted. 90 degrees Fahrenheit in a dark room was how most of my summers went.

Hostility was in control. My reality at home had manifested at summer school. I did not belong, yet I embraced it. With no reason to believe things would change, I accepted the dangerous conditions. Students were escorted around the building like trained animals. Fights broke out often as many kids were sent to the hospital. The only people in the entire building who were not black were upper administration. They were comfortable in their air-conditioned room away from the drama. I was used to seeing four gray walls for the first four hours of the day while the sun shined through the window-padded bars.

***

Gang members flooded the halls of the middle school I attended. Like most schools, it was a different world. You were grouped with those who best fit your socio-economic status and background. The socio-economic split was noticeable from the moment you walked in.

My school was separated by floors. The first floor had most of the upper-middle class white students. The second floor was a mixture of white and black students, middle class. The third and fourth floor were predominantly of minority population, lower-middle class. Black and brown urban youth, inner-city white kids, flooded those floors. Being on the third floor with Abdul exposed us to more gang affiliation and street life from sunup to sundown.

Middle school is an awkward phase of life for most. A strong majority of kids go through puberty and are bullied for features beyond their control. I found out all too quickly how many flaws I had when I was in middle school. Unable to buy my own clothes, I did not have "swag." My clothes were always made fun of. I was compared to the starving kids in Africa from my skinny body frame. In sixth grade, I started as a nobody looking to fit in.

***

In DC Universe comic-based film, The Dark Knight and the Dark Knight Rises there are villains within the movies that viewers seemed to understand better, when they knew their origin. Even though the Joker suffered severely as a child, but I relate more with Bane. Bane is the supervillain who showed that he could revolutionize the criminal underworld. One fight scene in the movie The Dark Knight Rises, Bane said, "You merely adopted the dark, I was born in it. Molded by it. I did not see the light until I was already a man…" He spent time in "the pit" for years as he became a supervillain from his experience.

As bad as my behavior was, it was a cry for acceptance. I desired loyalty. The other foster kids spoke to their mother weekly which proved their loyalty to her. The thought of possibly speaking to my biological mother crossed my mind. I felt like one of the mutants from the X-Men series. I did not belong. I felt like Magneto from the X-Men as he lost his mother as a child. When he attempted to recreate his life, he also lost the love of his life. All he knew was pain and hurt. In middle school, it was all I had to offer.

***

Middle school was that phase where you were labelled either "cool" or "corny." I drifted towards the street hustlas and gang members. One kid I kicked it with was far more superior than his fellow peers. He wore fresh clothes and only spoke when he was spoken to. His calm poise even made school officials respect him. He hardly disrespected anyone, as it was hard to tell he was gang affiliated. While gang members were shooting dice in the halls, he kept his distance.

His mysterious and quiet mannerism made him stand out among the loud and attention-seeking thugs. He distinguished himself from the rest of his crew. *I need that type of respect.* I thought. His name was Qway. It took a while, but I gained his loyalty and became his right-hand man in middle school. Qway's style of leadership was more appealing than JD's. JD did too many criminal activities to keep up with. Qway embodied the label of ghost. JD went to school when he wanted, but Qway attended school every day. JD actively recruited us boys in the house to be in the gang, while Qway attracted the qualities needed to be in that lifestyle.

Qway's presence ignited my once buried confidence as I began to form my identity. He enhanced my knowledge on the streets and watched my back. Confidence, being one of my natural gifts, flowed in school but I used it to flirt with girls. My confidence grew at the rate where self-sabotage was bound to happen.

At 11-years-old, flirting with girls was natural. I had a crush on a girl with long jet-black hair. She had a reddish-brown skin complexion. I saw her one-time during lunch and attempted to win her approval. I made fun of one of her guy friends when he attempted to assert himself. I took it disrespectfully and made fun of his physical features. Things escalated quickly. I made the girls laugh which angered him. I felt threatened so I grabbed a milk carton and threw it at him. He grabbed his own carton of milk and poured it on top of my head. It was my first suspension. Since I "brought the heat" I was the example of what happened when one of us "brought the heat" in foster care.

"If a flower bloomed in a dark room would you trust it?"

–Kendrick Lamar

We were home from school at 2:30 pm but none of us could have hobbies or extracurricular activities. The foster parents were creative with their punishment. Their "go to" was feeding me nasty food. The warden saw me drawing as I sat in the pit. He destroyed my drawings and threw them across the room. I was not allowed in my bed until 8:30pm, bedtime in middle school. Six hours on weekdays, I sat in "the pit."

On the weekends, the warden woke me up at 8:30am to send me to the pit until 8:30pm. The warden barged in our room every week, nearly breaking the door. On Saturday's and Sunday's, I sat on the steps from 8am until 8pm. His words, "Get ya a** on the steps!" Woke me every morning. At night he said, "Bedtime snake, get ya a** to that bed. The steps will wait for you in the morning." Anxiety filled my mind before the sun came up. I sat on the stairs for what felt like centuries. A few times per year, the warden gave me a day off for one of two reasons. It was either because he felt like being "nice" or when it was the holiday (typically New Year's).

The carpet on the stairs the rotted beneath me. He gave days off from the steps once every other month, plus holidays, which if I had to guess added up to a two-week calendar year worth of days in a 52-week calendar year. The other 50 weeks of the year, I sat in the pit. Haunted by the voices of oppression, I sat saturated with negative thoughts. Crying or making any noise was forbidden. Here is a breakdown of the number of hours spent sitting in the pit.

(Weekdays) 6 hours per day x 5 days per week =

30 hrs. per week.

(Weekends) 12 hours per day x 2 days per week =

24 hours per week.

30 hours + 24 hours =

54 hours per week.

54 hours per week x 50 weeks per year =

2,700 hours per year.

2,700 hrs. per year x 3 (middle school) years = 8,100 hours roughly spent on stairs at age 11, 12, and 13 years old. To give it context, there are 8,760 hours in a full calendar year. That is 8,100 hours of hearing voices, being stepped over, being called out my name. It fueled the suicidal thoughts. This is how Bane must have felt in "the pit." Those are key years to my brain development. That is how super villains are created.

The Pit

The 8,100 hours, included three Christmas's. I saw the excitement on everyone's face as they anticipated receiving many gifts. I received no gifts for three years. I was forced to go trick-or-treating on Halloween only to give all my candy to the other foster kids. I was always hungry, so I lived like the animal they treated me. I salvaged food from the garbage pails. Out of the hundreds of times, I ate out of trash cans and Aeisha was the only person who witnessed it.

She asked, "What are you doing?" I looked at her as she watched me stuff my face with my bare hands.

"You gonna snitch me out?" When she looked into my eyes, she felt my pain. Aeisha experienced her own trauma in foster care. All the pain she endured, she still managed to empathize. I cursed the day I came out of my mother's womb as did she as well.

"I am not interested in picking up crumbs of compassion thrown from the table of someone who considers himself my master. I want the full menu of rights."

-Desmond Tutu

Year after year, I suffered unjustly because instead of being corrected as a young black boy, I was severely disciplined for impulsive actions. I felt cheated and robbed me of the opportunity to have a real family. I created drawings and wrote stories about having a family, only for the warden to tell me "drawing is for sissies." He made me public enemy number one.

***

As I was treated as an outcast, Pepe was praised for good grades. Pepe walked up and down the stairs stepping right over me as if I was a disease that could not be touched. Pepe was more intuitive than me as his intelligence made us foster kids feel inferior to his superiority complex. In the black community, it was common to get into fights, if you showed yourself as being better than your community members.

While us I was learning how to be gangsters, Pepe kept his head in the books. He used his mind to his competitive advantage. His knowledge and use of versatile vocabulary made him first in line to be the warden's "go to" guy when JD was finally kicked out the house. Pepe gained authority under the warden's wing.

The more neglected I felt within the house, the bigger my need came for acceptance from my street homies. Abdul reported everything I did in school. Explaining myself became counterproductive. I lost the desire to get back to their "good side." At-11 years-old, as I declared my loyalty to the crew I rolled with in school. *Damned if I do, damned if I do not so I might as well do what I want.*

In the house, I was blamed for missing food, broken furniture, destroying other people's property, then beat into a "forced confession." Out of the six foster kids in the house between the ages of 10 and 15, I took the fault. The warden ensured order in his chaotic household, which gave opportunity for us prisoners to take advantage of those with no voice.

***

In the pit, I had nightmares of the gingerbread man attacking me.

When I awoke, the nightmares were my reality.

Sleeping did not stop the nightmares. Neither did my conscious mind.

Were the nightmares a mirror of my reality, or the other way around?

Fear kept the pain internal if I was inexpressive.

The gingerbread man attached after I got in trouble.

He always took my mind off the misery of the pit.

You see the gingerbread man could not be caught.

He was too crafty and outwitted the devil.

He was a slick talker.

I yelled, screamed, and cried on the inside for someone to come to my rescue.

The closet was always dark, but my mind was darker.

I was 9 years old when it happened.

The trouble I caused were siren and bells going off.

It was the gingerbread man.

He went away for a couple of days and returned when he pleased.

Why?

It was the gingerbread man.

Threats were no good to the gingerbread man.

"Would anyone believe you?"

He was right. It was the gingerbread man.

His influence was second to the warden.

I fought with the laws that governed my mind and my body.

He could not be caught.

He could not be tamed.

Like most unwelcome guest, he left a trail of pain.

***

Middle school was all about the art of fight, flight, or freeze. Who I hung around determined my response. Hanging around gangsta's and goons kept my head on a swivel. Most of the guys I hung around had fearless attitudes, but any moment was life or death. I went to school to look for items to steal like a sniper looking at his target through a scope on a rifle gun. That is how I originated my tag name "SDot." Stealing was only surface level, I had much to learn about the game. I did any and everything to catch someone slipping.

I stole items of monetary value like wallets, money clips, phones and other electronic devices like iPod. Back then, none of the items were traceable like they are in today's world. Back in 2006-2007, Motorola Razor phones, Boost Mobile Chirp phones, and first-generation iPod were all popular trending items that I sold for a couple extra dollars.

Qway, like many of my friends growing up, was born into the hustla's lifestyle. Gaining his trust was no easy task as he was heavily guarded and did not let his walls down. He trusted me enough to break down the rules of what it meant to "put in" work and show loyalty. One of the rules I kept in high regard was "Loyalty over royalty." Stealing from those closest to you was asking for trouble. It created distrust and if you cannot be trusted, you were a liability. They say there is no honor among thieves, I certainly beg to differ.

I never stole from my classmates. I had more loyalty from my classmates than I did in my own household. Loyalty was rarely spoken at the foster house. Us foster children took the local bus route to school as we pretended to be "family." The warden had a fantasy philosophy of us being a "unit" or a "gang," he suggested that we referred to the other foster siblings as "family." His words fell on deaf ears as the division within the house led to us being divided outside the house. A divided house cannot stand. We were as divided as the Japs and the American's after the Pearl Harbor bombings.

We each deserved Emmy awards for the front we put on based on the horrors we faced at home. During middle school, no one rebelled as much as I did. My boldness became a liability to the warden's system as I distanced myself from the other foster children. The warden rewarded them with snacks and other incentives as they reported my gang activity.

Controlled by anger

All the built-up anger and frustration made me a "hot head." A teacher I disliked felt the need to pick on me often. She spoke to me as if she was above me. She reminded me of the warden, so I was rebellious in her class.

One time she said, "Another word from you and I'll throw you out of here, you hear me!?" It triggered the emotions I had harbored inside of me. My blood boiled from her threatening words. I blanked out. Out of anger, the next words nearly tossed me in jail as I threatened the lives of everyone in the school. The class erupted into laughter in a momentum shift. That moment seemed to be what I needed to retaliate against her threatening words. The look on her face gave me the satisfaction of retaliation. Unfortunately for me, she had the last laugh. The exact moment the class calmed down, as if it were scripted out of a movie, the dean casually walked into the class and stood by the door with his arms crossed over his chest.

The teacher stared into my soul with the look of revenge as I froze in the moment of eye contact. She walked over to where the dean stood and whispered in his ear. His eyes locked on my little posture as I anticipated the worst-case scenario. My mind raced as thousands of negative thoughts swarmed my imagination. The class sat in dead silence as tension filled the room. *There was no way out of this one.* Anxiety kicked in as I was trapped. My heart stopped for a split second as the dean took me to the office. An hour went by and two police officers in full NYPD uniform entered the office.

The dean explained, "these two officers were sent to take you into custody. Threats to public property is an act of domestic terrorism and is subjected to severe consequences. Do you know how serious your threat is being taken especially post 9/11?"

"Now," the Dean continued. "I spoke to your foster parents about your situation and they mentioned how you are a foster child and they suggested that I allow them handle it instead of taking you into custody. The warden and I have an agreement not to arrest you if you did not cause any more trouble." His words fell on deaf ears.

The thought of the warden beating me up made my body tense. The warden whooped me when I entered his house. I did not have a chance to blink before his hand slapped me across my face as my head hit the floor. "Get up!" He boomed. I held my swollen cheek. I stood to my feet trembling. Another slap to the face, this time I stumbled and managed to catch my footing. Another slap to the face, and another one. He grabbed his belt that was right next to his chair hanging on the banister and whipped me for what felt like forever. It was one of those "black parenting" moments where the whole house heard the child screaming for dear life.

The warden's tactics to whip me into obedience was futile as I continued to disobey his words. I recited the gang's creed to keep me motivated. The warden knew I was gang affiliated and threw haymakers at me as the other foster kids watched in awe. I threw up gang signs in school and the warden boxed me at his house. It was too late, mentally I purposely ignored his commands.

Chapter 5: The Real Sanctuary

My unfair treatment shaped my view on God. Our perception of the Heavenly Father can be based on how we see our early guardians. To me, God was punishing and unforgiving. Attending church was not a practice in my household. If God truly existed, I believe He hated me. I wanted no part of a "loving" God that allowed me to suffer for situations beyond my control.

How do I believe in a Heavenly Father that allows me to suffer this much? No matter what the warden thought about me, I did not deserve his treatment. I attended youth group with Pepe as a reason to get out of the house. Given my situation, the youth pastor's words went in one ear and out the other. My life was loveless. I went through the prayers, went to the altar calls, and confessed my sins in attempts to be "Godly." It did me no good. My reality was confined to a prison home. Seeking God in four walls of a church was ineffective.

I did not know God's will, did not follow His commandments, and did not know the Lord's prayer.

"You'll be going to hell if you don't act right and believe in God." They said.

To me, I was already living in hell. My mind replayed the terrible events in my life like a horror film. *Why not just end my life for good since all I cause is pain?* Fear had planted its seeds as the most awful thoughts came to mind as I sat in church.

At times, my heart responded to the voice of Fear by replaying the words the youth pastor spoke. When sermons popped in my mind, I opened the Bible and read it every now and again. Reading the bible was oddly satisfying. At times, it even made me feel hopeful in the pit.

Nothing to lose

I was forbidden to go to the neighborhood park by myself. The park was known as "yard time." Most of the foster kids were home bodies but Pepe went to the park as often as possible. Pepe, being skinny with a lanky body, was an incredible basketball player. The other basketball players respected his skills. His performance on the court made him shine. It was one of the rare times he ever smiled.

One day I challenged him one vs one to prolong going back to the pit. My motivation to play basketball did not come from the game, but from the desire to stay out of that house. After months of competing against Pepe and the other neighborhood kids, my body began to form into that of a street hooper. The definition from my muscles began to form early in life. My hate for life transitioned to the love for basketball. The more I lost, the hungrier I became to win. I developed the killer instinct of a lion. Pepe was like the golden unicorn that the lion only dreamed of catching. The further the unicorn ran, the more determined I was to catch it.

The countless days, weeks, and months of basketball created a "nothing to lose mentality." I played with a chip on my shoulder. I tasted the blood of the golden unicorn when I beat Pepe for the first time. Out brotherhood was disregarded on the court, I was out to rip his head off his shoulders.

My "nothing to lose" mentality propelled me to dominate Pepe and many others in basketball. Basketball was my way to cope with life. The court became my sanctuary and the only place I felt free to express my anger and frustration. Basketball was my ticket out of my reality as my thoughts became less negative after playing basketball. Every time I went back into the prison from the park, I was reminded of my worthlessness.

We walked into the house and Pepe was asked the same two questions.

"How was the park?"

Pepe's answer never changed, "good." Details were never given.

"Did Schwartzen steal or do anything stupid," followed by the death glare directed at me.

"No," Pepe answered. It was routine. I sat on the stairs mentally projecting myself back on the courts. The mental picture was my sanctuary. It gave me hope that *maybe I was meant to play basketball if I made it to the age of 18.*

*** *

Living in isolation from the rest of the foster kids became second nature. I accepted the malnourishment of my body and emotions as I endured the abuse. There came a time when I was asked if I ever wanted to get out of "the pit." My answer was "no." I was content with life in the pit. If I were to escape, it would be on my own terms. Pit or sympathy was the last thing I needed. The thought of liberating myself was my driving force. It became the hope I needed not to follow through with my suicidal thoughts.

I can be free from the terrible names, free from the lies, free from the labels, free from the gangs, free from the life I was forced to live. One day I can be free to choose my own life, choose what time I went to bed, free to choose what I wanted to eat when I wanted to eat it. The feeling of freedom filled me with peace. The peace I sought to obtain was stronger than my problems in foster care. I prayed for the voice of truth to be heard.

Chapter 6: Dark Leadership

"I am a leader by default, only because nature does not allow a vacuum."

-Desmond Tutu

By age 13, my mind was fixed in the hustla's lifestyle. My thoughts were hardwired by street code. My actions were driven through the amount of money I could make. Youngers kids looked to me as their leader as I had them out stealing for me. My entire influence was dominated by thugs, goons, and goblins. I learned the hard way that one wrong moment of peer pressure can change your life forever.

At the end of science class one day, some classmates and I clowned around near the teacher's desk. I was being a clown and went through her desk. What I found took me by surprise. Her pocketbook was in one of the drawers. In a split second, one of my classmates looked and said, "yo SDot, take her sh*t son."

"Nah man, you take it."

"You right there son. Hurry up she might come back."

The voice of truth boomed as clear as day. *It is not for the gang and it's not for yourself. This is for a couple of clowns having fun. Chill out, close the drawer, and walk away.* I closed the drawer without touching her bag.

"You a punk, son, I thought you were down with that gang you be bangin." The classmate provoked me.

"What!?" I said as I looked at him sideways.

"Go, go, go, and hurry! Someone's coming back." My classmate rushed.

The words struck my ego; my reputation was on the line. Fear decided to speak to me in the moment. *If you do not take it word would get out that you punked out of stealing. Your reputation is on the line.* I opened the drawer, opened her pocketbook and opened the wallet full of cash. My heartbeat increased. *Do not take it,* the voice of truth said. I panicked and grabbed a handful of cash. I closed the bottom drawer and ran out of the classroom.

My classmate said, "yo, give me some cash."

They laughed as they galloped through the hallway full of excitement. The moment they spotted Qway, they told him. The crime I committed made me feel powerful. I felt respected. I was face to face with Qway, the person I had put in work for the past two years. I grew from under his wing and was ready to spread my own wings. Little did I know, it took less than 24 hours for an investigation to begin on the money I stole.

***

The next day school officials called each of my classmates to the office throughout the school day. Finally, I had been called into the office. The dean and the assistant principal wasted no time.

"Eyewitnesses say you stole the money from Ms. C's pocketbook."

"Well your eyewitnesses are wrong. You can't prove anything." I gave no second thought to confessing. The school officials did not entertain my denials. After determined efforts of threats of expulsion, I continued to deny all accusations. The dean threatened to call the warden.

"Call him!" I was fed up. The student who told me to steal the money entered the office.

"It comes down to you both. One of you took the money and if one of you confesses the other will be in no trouble. If neither of you confess both of you will be expelled." It was a major ultimatum. After we both denied accusations, the assistant principal turned it over to the head principal. I prepared for expulsion. My classmate was in full panic mode as I walked through the hallway like a prisoner on death row.

My classmate begged me to tell the truth. His words made me stop and think. I figured I'd give it a shot and if I was expelled, so be it. I went up to the assistant principal and told them the truth about stealing the money. I was escorted to the principal's office as the other student was told to go back to class. I sat in their office as he pulled out a folder that contained my records, grades, and previous suspensions. As he read them, he spoke.

"Your grades are good Schwartz; you do not seem like the type of kid to do something like this. What happened?" My eyes locked on the floor. I felt ashamed as my body sunk into the couch.

"I took some money from the teacher's purse."

"We have to suspend you of course, but my policy says for something like this is grounds for expulsion." He continued, "Schwartz, you have to…" and I disregarded his words. *These people do not care about you; it's their job to get rid of you. You are nothing but trouble and the warden is going to snap you in half when you get to his house.*

Instead of being expelled, I was given a week suspension. I was dismissed as word travelled throughout the school that I robbed a teacher. I was presented with gang beads shortly after. I figured this would be the last straw to get kicked me out of the house. I was ready. As soon as I stepped into the house, I told the warden what happened. I did not know where I would go. He had been threatening to kick me out for years. The thought of being homeless made my hands numb, my feet heavy and my belly sink. *Where would I live? What would I eat?* I held onto my gang beads and reminded myself that the streets were where I belonged.

I approached the warden when I walked into the house. With no hesitation, I told him how I stole money from the teacher. The warden tackled me mid story as his hands wrapped around my neck as he threw me against the sofa.

"Stop! Stop! Let the boy finish his story." His wife said in a frenzy.

I continued to tell them I was suspended for a week and school officials wanted to meet with them.

"Go grab his book bag Abdul!" The warden boomed. Abdul rummaged through my book bag and presented my gang beads to the warden.

"They're gang beads," Abdul said with no hesitation. "All the gang members around school wear them."

The warden boxed me in my chest. I attempted to protect myself from his left hooks. He beat me as a grown man beats another grown man and sent me to the pit when he was done.

"Get ready to pack your bags, Sparford and Rikers will be your new home soon!"

Weeks went by and I still lived in his house. The warden lost the power behind his words as he did not follow through. His words were empty. His threats went in vain. I endured his punches as my body grew stronger. His punches were less painful. I was suspended a few more times and got used to the suspension room. I was feared. As a young black male growing up watching black cinemas, being feared was a way of being respected.

The teacher I stole from failed me every report card grade. She was unafraid to show her hate towards me. I tried what I thought could make the situation better. One day I sat in the pit and wrote her an apology letter and presented it to her after class. She asked to speak to me about the letter. I refused to look into her eyes. She had a simple request, a sit down between her, me, the foster parents, and the dean. They say it never hurts to ask a question, but in that household, asking for permission was worse than asking for forgiveness. The warden had no tolerance for what he called "stupidity." The foster parents denied my request to meet with the teacher. There was no hope for redemption.

I developed my core crew and put them to work. I stepped up my street game by carrying guns and knives. I remember the first time I held a gun. It was heavy and the weight of the gun in my hand made me feel powerful. Eventually, I obtained my own gun since the rush I felt from the sleek trigger against my index finger gave me power. Building a life outside of my foster home was easy since no one truly cared. Every day I arrived home, the warden forced me to turn my book bag inside out. His methods became counterproductive as he drilled me with questions.

"What did you steal today?"

"Who did you lie to?"

"Did you get high?"

"Are you hiding drugs upstairs?"

"Did you rob any teachers?"

The more he questioned me, the less control he had. Five years living with the warden and my face was stone cold. It was like tying my shoe, too easy. He caught me slipping one day. During one of his interrogations, he sent Abdul to seize my possessions in a secluded part of the closet. As Abdul rummaged through my possessions and found several pocketknives. When he brought the knives downstairs, my heart jumped as Fear spoke, *If Abdul finds the money and gun you have hidden, you must run out the house.*

"What is this for!?" The warden demanded.

"Protection," I answered. The warden followed up with a left hook to the face and I fell to the ground.

"You brought this in my damn house!?" The warden proceeded to stomp on me as I laid on the floor. He sent Abdul back upstairs to search through my possession again.

"See if you can find a gun Abdul, keep looking!" After 10 minutes of searching, he found nothing else. When I went in the closet to check if my money was still there, it was. As a last resort, I prayed to God. I asked Him to take me away from this place. My desire was to run away and never come back.

***

I had my crew set up Abdul to make his brand-new coat disappear. I had to quench my thirst for revenge since he found those knives. I gathered my crew together at school and gave them the assignment. The next day at lunch, my crew executed the plan exactly how I pictured it. I felt like a coach watching his team execute plays written out in the playbook. Like a retired gymnast watching their apprentice do the exact moves they had taught them in practice. The sweet smell of revenge. Abdul went home at the end of the day without his expensive coat.

I kept a close eye on Abdul to see if he was going to retaliate. Abdul was no punk but at the same time, we watched each other's moves. Inside the house, I was powerless but outside the house, I had "juice" and the ability to make things happen. The war between us raged as we tussled in the school hallway. We were far from brothers. The warden decided to send Abdul and I to the same high school. He thought sending me to a suburban school would keep me away from the street life. He was wrong by a long shot. I attended the only public high school in Staten Island that wore uniform.

***

The summer before I entered high school, I hustled to keep money in my pockets. As a 14-year-old young black male, school was last on my priority list. Education was no means to success to me since was surrounded myself with dope dealers and hustlas. My vision was bound by my environment.

The high school I attended had to be the smallest NYC high school in 2008 during its inaugural year. My class was the first class of students at the school. There were no upperclassmen and most teachers had no prior experience. The only aspect of the school I was impressed by was the basketball courts.

Out of the 120 students in its inaugural year, roughly 80% of the students were Italian or of Caucasian descent. It was my first time being in a predominantly white environment. Being from a middle school with 2,000+ students where I hung with gangstas and hustlas was no easy transition. The voices of the household I was in boomed in my mind as I saw the white students interacting with one another. *Stay away from white people. Stay away from white people.*

There were no graffiti on desks or walls, very minimal gang activity and the social influence did not come from hustlas. I experienced severe anxiety, as my mind attempted to adapt. Not being able to rob or hustle in school threw me off. If stealing was my drug of choice, I experienced withdrawals. Being exposed to violence so many years made me carry weapons to school even though I was not in any immediate danger.

I was glad to reunite with my grade school friends, including A-Will. He grew to 6'0 200lbs but still had a baby face. Seeing him reminded me of how much I had changed. A-Will was the friend who always made you laugh. A-Will knew about my street life but never judged me. He had an eye for great basketball talent as well. His level of respect towards my basketball skills was greater than his respect for me as a survivalist.

I felt like I was being watched at school. I thought everyone around me saw me as a criminal. The non-hostile environment was awkward since I had limited access to trouble. All I thought about in school was basketball. Every lunch hour during school for four years I was on that court. Everyone knew me as the basketball "jock," but I looked at myself as a criminal.

The first goal I set in high school was to make the varsity team as a freshman. The varsity basketball team was shared between the two schools combined into one program. After staying away from trouble for a few months, I spoke to the coach who spoke to the warden which granted me permission to attend tryouts. The warden did not believe I was good enough to make the team. He sent Abdul to babysit me at my workouts and tryouts.

Even though I lacked the fundamentals of basketball, my tenacious spirit impressed the coaches. I had no prior organized basketball experience. I soaked up every bit of criticism the coaches gave me. The basketball terminology was foreign to me as I felt like a small fish in a large pond. My determination pushed me through tryouts, and I became the first Gaynor Mccown student to make the College of Staten Island High school (CSI) /MCcown varsity basketball team as a freshman.

The excitement was short lived as the warden refused to pay $250 in team fees. He slapped me across the face for asking him what he called "a dumb a** question." My varsity experience as a freshman was gone in a moment. That moment did something to my spirit and erupted a part of me that had been waiting to come out since the day I entered the warden's house in March 2003.

Chapter 7: Escape from Alcatraz

*"Nobody can give you freedom. Nobody can give you equality,
justice, or anything. If you're a man, you take it."* –Malcolm X

With the absence of basketball, I drifted back to survival
mode. One day in March 2009, I walked through the hallway
passing a student who placed a Sidekick 3 phone in their locker.
I sat in class and thought anxiously on how I needed to take their
phone. My body quivered as I felt like a dope fiend missing the
high. During a bathroom break, I sprang into action. I walked up
the locker and yanked on the lock as it opened with ease. I
placed the phone in my pocket and calmly walked away. I went
back to class and before the day ended, I was asked to report to
the office. I walked into the dean's office calm as ever. The dean
was a bald Italian man, mid 30's 5'8, with a cheesy go-tee.

"Where's the phone Schwartz," he asked me as I took a
seat.

"What phone?" This was not my first rodeo, but I was a
bad liar.

"Listen, you can sit here and play dumb all you want,
but we both know you have the phone." As he spoke, a security
guard entered the office and shut the door behind him.

After going back and forth, he turned the computer monitor on his desk to face toward me. It was as if I was staring into another dimension. Clear as day, it showed my 5'9 135lb body frame walking up to the locker, yanking the lock, placing the phone in my pocket and calmly walking away. The level of comfort I had reached with stealing blew my mind. I did not see anything wrong with stealing until that moment. Fate showed to be faithful as I saw the young black male on the TV screen for the first time. *Could this be what the warden and everyone in the household sees every day?* It was my wake-up call. My eyes were glued to the screen as the dean played the video again. *Is that how my head looks on camera? I guess it really is big.*

The Dean spoke, "Here's what's going to happen, the security guard will escort you to wherever you're hiding the phone and you will bring it back to the office." I did exactly what he said and was hit with a week's suspension. The chains of disillusionment fell off as the moment of escape had presented itself. All the money I saved over the years was in my locker. After six long years of rebellion and surviving in the trenches of a terrible foster home, it was time for me to get away for good.

If I can start my life over at 8-years-old with only a suitcase and the clothes on my back, I can start my life over at 14-years-old with a pocket full of money. I was unable to determine if it was fear or truth speaking. I did not go to the foster house after school. I contacted one of my homies from middle school; we hopped on the bus and went off into the night. The unfamiliar winter wind blew chills as we exited the bus and entered an unfamiliar neighborhood.

I was welcomed into my homie's house by a scent of incense burning on his beige wall. The beige wall matched the beige carpet. His living room was neatly decorated with paintings, a couch, bookshelves, and a large flat screen TV that caught the attention of anyone who walked through the front door. I took a seat as my homie spoke with his mom in the kitchen. *I am here?* The voice of liberation felt amazing to hear. *I did it. I am never going back to that house. No one will miss me anyways.* My inner dialogue was interrupted by the introduction of my homie's mom. After some small talk, she left her son and I together.

"What you gonna do son?" He asked.

"I told you already, I'll hook up with my crew from middle school and go from there," I said sure of myself. Before he asked another question, his phone played a Kayne West song:

"In the night, I hear em' talk,

the coldest story ever told,

somewhere far along the road he lost his soul,

to a woman so heartless."

The song lyrics that captured my feelings at that moment, heartless. My homie's brown face turned pale as he read the message from his Sidekick 2008.

"Son, they're looking for you." His tone expressed second thoughts about permitting me in his home. I voluntarily decided it was time to leave.

"How am I supposed to get in contact with my homies if I gotta leave? Where am I going to go?" My voice calmly asked. He paced back and forth with his fingers locked on top of his head that showed his anxiety.

"I can't have the cops come to my crib yo, I told my mom you were a good friend staying over, but if they come here, she's gonna beat my a** bro." His words hit deep. The last thing I wanted was to cause harm to another household.

"Alright fam, I'll leave for tonight just in case the cops come and then I'll meet you at the park in the morning around 10am, that's cool?"

"Alright, that works, but where you are going tonight then?"

"Lemme use ya phone right quick."

I used his phone to contact my homies from middle school. He lived in the neighborhood close to my homie. As soon as I left his house, the strong winter wind nearly knocked me over. I carried my book bag, a light jacket and the school uniform that I wore to school that day. I was on my own. My mind fixed on freedom, as I could not imagine sitting in the pit ever again. *Anything was better than going back to that house;* the truth spoke loud and clear.

I walked into a black gated community where four large buildings stood 13 stories tall. The gate entrance lock had been broken off. There was graffiti on the walls and in the lobby of the building. As I took the elevator to the ninth floor, I imagined the countless number of fights, shootouts, robberies that took place. It felt as if I arrived at the Promised Land. I stepped off the elevator and noticed the bullet holes in the glass windows at both ends of the hallway. Chills ran through my body as I imagined someone dying in the exact spot. My homie invited me in as I explained my situation.

"Man," he spoke as he shook his head. "This ain't the life you want SDot, fa real. You better off going back to that foster house. This life will lead you down a path no one wants to be on. Qway put you down with us cause you had heart. You did crazy sh*t in school SDot. It was fun and games in school, but in these streets SDot, man it's life or death, kill or be killed. You wanna live like that?"

We were interrupted by a knock on the door. He grabbed his .380 gun and asked who it was. It was some of the homies from the gang.

"SDot, what you doing here?" Another gang member recognized me right away.

Before I could answer, my homie did. "SDot ran away from his home son, I'm tellin' the lil homie to go back."

Mid conversation, more guys from the gang showed up. After about 10 minutes, we began smoking weed and clowning one another. It was laughs and good vibes, what I needed after a stressful day. I imagined fighting, dice games, loud music from based on how they acted at school. There was no tension, no stress, no arguing, just jokes and some bragging rights about whose girl looked better. When they all left, BLove and I went back into his apartment.

"Ima hook you up with some food and kick you out because if the cops come here lookin' for you. Ima say I ain't seen you." He spoke with sincerity.

The drama from the day wore off as I sobered from the cold blowing winter wind. I walked the streets of Staten Island aimlessly for what seemed like hours. I decided to walk to a familiar park in attempts to sleep. When I arrived, there were four Mexican men sleeping on the bench and on the gates that surrounded the park. I was used to sleeping on hard rotten stairs, so a wooden bench was not so different. I sat on the bench only to be disrupted by the noise of the wind blowing through the leaves. The wind prevented me from sleeping. I walked to the local 24-hour supermarket in attempts to sleep.

I walked into the supermarket and sat on the bench. It was quiet, the lights were bright but at least I was warm. Two middle aged white men sat down, and I sat next to them. I could not help but listen to the conversation about basketball knowing I was forbidden to play on my varsity team. I looked around to see the night crew unpacking boxes while the soothing music from the speakers rocked my eyelids closed. I dozed off, kicked my feet up on the bench and woke up seven hours later to the birds chirping right outside the supermarket.

I woke up energized and ready for my life as an outlaw. I met up with my homie that allowed me to see some of my old crew. My homie, Baker, agreed for me to stay with him. He was 6'2 and had a mean left hook. He punched me one time in 8th grade. He had a place in we crashed at. We went to his place to change clothes and went out to one of Staten Island's most gang infested movie theaters on Forest Avenue. The Forest avenue movies were known for shootouts, fights, and gang wars. A couple of my homies from school met up with us that night.

That night I knew I needed a cellphone. I scanned the sea of people in the parking lot of the theater. I looked for someone to rob. The fellas clowned me about how I never learned my lesson.

"How you lookin' to steal again after that's why you ran away in the first place SDot?"

They were right, but I brushed their words off and found my targets. I noticed two white teenage males that both had Sidekick cell phones.

"Aye fellas watch this," indicating I was up to something.

I slowly crept up on the boys as they were near some parked cars in the lot. I ran up to them and landed a clean punch to the face. Immediately, he stumbled and fell back as his friend took off running. I grabbed the guy by his coat, threw him up against the car demanding his phone. My fists clenched his shirt as my knuckles were against his chin, neck, and chest. Fear filled his soul as I could see the reflection of my face through his blue eyes.

He pulled out his Sidekick Slide and handed it to me. I pushed him away with a force that made him stumble as he ran off. I came back to my senses. My heart raced; the robbery felt better than blindly stealing. The rush made me feel powerful, like the gangsta's on TV. I walked back to the group and as they laughed hysterically.

"I told y'all to watch, right?" I felt like a champion, like I accomplished something significant. The homies praised me. The rest of the night I was paranoid by the thought of retaliation. I anxiously left the movie theater and I smoked to clear my mind. Spending weeks in a trap house made me come across people that lived as serial criminals. I met professional con artists who made a living off scamming and dealing.

"Don't get caught slippin'. Everyone in the hood is looking to catch a come up."

As I was out in the streets with my homies, I received an instant message. The warden's wife message me saying the detectives were looking for me. I replied saying I was never coming back.

"Yo, my adopted moms texted me son." Baker looked at me and asked me what she said. After texting back and forth, the bus route we took began to approach the stop to get off at the warden's house.

"You think I should go back? My adopted mom said we can figure this out together and we can talk about it." Baker suggested for me to go home.

As the bus stopped at my home stop, I took one-step forward to get off the bus. Time slowed down. The rain poured down heavy as I watch the water slide down the public bus window. It was as if the bus driver had stopped purposefully for me to go back to the warden's house. The roaring engine sound disappeared as if the bus was out of service. *Had the bus driver turned the bus off?*

I snapped out of the moment by the eruption of memories of fear at the warden's house that I knew scarred my mental abilities. *I cannot go back. That life was too sickening.* My truth spoke clearly. I did not expect anyone to understand the years of suffering I endured. I stayed on the bus and began to live my life as the hustla I was trying to be.

***

While a runaway, I always saw my girl, Lady Twin. She was a cute Puerto Rican girl that had my back on the streets. She lived in my neighborhood and was my informant on the block. She kept an eye out for me in the streets. I visited Lady Twin over a dozen times as a runaway. Her loyalty served me greatly as she ran the risk of trouble to kick it with me.

The trap house Baker and I stayed at eventually got shut down. The day it was shut down we walked to a gas station where I found a car that had the driver's door unlocked. We were on his way to his mother's house, but I brought the stolen goods from the car to her house. She flipped out on the both of us.

"Get in my room right now!" She boomed to Baker.

Baker went to her room and she yelled like any concerned parents would. I was unsure of how to muster up the courage to tell her I was a runaway.

"How long do you plan to stay in my house? You're not only Baker's responsibility if I allow you to stay here but mine too."

I did not know what to say. I stared at her with the blank expression. She looked right in my eyes and asked me the question of a lifetime.

"Are you a runaway Schwartz?"

My head went down immediately as the eye contact became intimidating. I was emotionally exposed.

"Yeah," I said as I stared down at the wooden floor.

"Don't be ashamed Schwartz, I ran away from home myself when I was a teenager."

My head lifted with great curiosity, "you did?"

"Oh yeah," she continued, "I had to. People in my house were sexually assaulting me for years and I had to get out. I ran away to live with friends until I bought my own place."

My eyes locked in on her face as her words were like fresh water in a dry desert to hear an adult talk about their own experience. She spoke fearlessly about her times she screwed up as a teenager. I stayed at her house for a few weeks until I decided to attend Baker's school. All my street homies attended the same school, as it was known for producing well known kingpins.

I walked in the school building and was met with massive groups of urban students. It reminded me of middle school. I noticed the bloods, crips, and local street gangs gambling in the hallways. I greeted all my homies and attempted to go to class. Teachers did not recognize me, and I pretended to be in the wrong class. I was left alone in the middle of the hallway.

I walked through the hallways a loud, "hey, why are you not in class?" A Puerto Rican man about 5 '7 with a round shaped body dressed in full security uniform stood only two feet to the right of me. I attempted to think of something to say but my mind drew a blank. I took notice of the exit door. *I could outrun this guy no problem*, I thought. Before I could say or do anything, he told me to follow him. My body felt as if it were in a trance. I walked with the security guard as he led the way to the principal's office. It was the end of the road.

The school officials interrogated me and minutes later, my adopted parents were on the phone. School officials found out I was a runaway. With three security guards in the room, I assumed I was being arrested. Sure enough, some time passed bye and two NYPD officers entered the office. They patted me down for contraband me until the warden and his wife arrived. The officers placed me in handcuffs and escorted me out of the principal's office and into a squad car. Being escorted out of the building in handcuffs by police officers made me feel like I was walking down the red carpet. It felt like a rite of passage as the cuffs squeezed my wrists. I kept my chin up. The officers walked me to the patty wagon. Right before I climbed in, we were interrupted by a soft-spoken individual.

"Officer, that's my foster child, do you mind if I say something to him first."

They granted the warden's wife permission. They turned me around and my eyes locked on hers. It felt like I had seen her for the first time. She wore an oversized big brown coat as the collar smothered her neck and cheeks with expensive fur.

"Schwartz," the wife started," Did you really think you were going to get away with this?" She looked me right in the eyes. "Mmmmm, mmmm, mmmm," she said while shaking her head.

"You've ruined your life, JD number 2." The tears rolled down my face unintentionally. It felt as if she had tried to trigger an emotion that was permanently numb. I bled on the inside while the tears slowly ran down my cheeks. I looked over in the warden's direction as he gave me the death glare. No words, but his face said it all. I climbed in the patty wagon and we drove off.

I stared out the window during the ride to the precinct. The officers cracked jokes as I looked up at the clouds to see how beautiful the sun looked in the clear blue sky. Despite being in handcuffs, in a van full of NYPD officers going down to the precinct, all I noticed was the sun. I stared at it, and it stared at me. My thoughts felt clear, I no longer felt anxious, I felt at peace. As the van arrived at the precinct, the sun was covered by the clouds.

Young black boy

I was placed in holding while cuffed to a steel bar. Not sure of the duration of time but the officers took me out of holding and escorted me to the back of a police vehicle. We drove to a facility called Bayley Seton. I anticipated the facility to be my new home. I felt the energy of the juvenile detention center as soon as I stepped through the manual automated doors. My time as an outlawed runaway black boy had come to an end.

I was the facility where black teenage boys who were brought up in the system spent their adulthood. *Now was not the time to be weak-minded.* The system had prepared me for this lifestyle. No freedom of thought or self-expression. The white walls in the facility along with the white coats that the staff wore spoke volumes. This was the step right before being fully incarcerated.

I was a ward of the state, another black boy lost in the broken system. I was just another black boy enslaved by social oppression without given a fair chance. At that moment, I thought about who my birth parents were. My dreams as a young black boy were limited to my environment. Just another black boy who was looking for love in all the wrong places. Just another black boy who ran the streets looking for acceptance hoping not to be arrested. No one at home cared about the traumas I endured as a young black boy. Just another black boy who cried for years, but no one cared about the young black boys' tears.

Just another black boy paying the sins of their parents. Just another black boy who needed his father, better yet a friend, to know he was loved. That is a narrative of how black boys in America grow up. Why should mine be any different? My behavior justified I was a criminal, a menace to society with all his other boyz in the hood. Just another black boy who thirsted for that Juice with his mind on some dead presidents. That's just the way it is for us impoverished black boys in America.

I sat in an all-white room with chairs around the surrounding wall. The single sided mirror reminded me of an interrogation room from the movies. An officer came into the room to unlock my handcuffs; my wrists were red and sore. The officer left the room as three adults walked into the room. I assumed they were counselors or psychiatrist of some sort since they each had a clipboard in their hand. One was a black male; one was a lady that looked to be of white or middle eastern descent and the last was an upper middle-aged white man.

They sat right in front of me to ask me questions. I was prepped for this part known as "psychological evaluation" I saw it from a show called "The Wire." One episode of the wire had teenage black boys being questioned in a room moments before sentencing to determine how much medication dosage they needed while they were in juvenile detention. I answered their questions truthfully. One question popped that became a moment of truth.

"Why do you feel that you were subjected to jail your entire life?"

"Ever since I came to the warden's household, I've been looked at as the problem child. Between Stony Large, Bailey Seaton, Sparford, Rikers Island (all detention centers across New York State) I've been told every day for the last six years it is where I'll be as an adult. What do you expect me to think? That's the future the system painted for me. You sit across from me in your fancy white clothes, clipboards, and pens knowing I'm not a threat to any of you. Your eyes tell it all, you have a job to do and I understand that. I'd rather run the risk of living on the streets than going to jail. Now tell me, what would you have done if you were in a position like mine?"

Silence. The black man in the white clothes that wore glasses had his eyes locked on my face. They wrote their last notes, thanked me for cooperating, and left the room. Minutes later, a police officer entered the room. I anticipated going on the detention center bus. *Say goodbye to anyone you've ever loved,* fear had its final words.

***

Young black boys were given no sympathy from the system. The officer placed me in handcuffs and escorted me out of the room. It was the end of the road. Before being placed on the bus, I had one more sit down. I sat down with doctors, counselors, and to my surprise, the warden and his wife entered the room. *I don't want to say goodbye to them, I want to say goodbye to my brother. Where is Trivet?* The voice of truth asked.

The doctor spoke.

"Schwartzen, the plan is to keep you hear at Bayley Seton hospital where you would be treated for your psychiatric condition (Fancy talk for the fact that I was messed up). Due to no prior criminal record, you are not subjected to juvenile detention. However, you are charged with trespassing on school property. You are adopted parents were given the option of a fine, community service or an assigned probation officer. The warden's wife sees fit that you be checked into Bayley Seton Hospital and to be treated accordingly. The warden overruled her request after hearing the overview of what life is like at Bailey Seton. He suggested with proper supervision of the probation officer with the agreement of weekly check-ins for a full year would fit you best."

Before the last words came out of her mouth, the officer in the room took the handcuffs off my wrists. I was caught off guard. The lady was a family court judge. I turned my head to look at the warden who gave me the death glare as the meeting ended. I stared at the warden with my poker face. *What just happened?* The warden and I signed paperwork as I were assigned a probation officer. The judge escorted me, the warden, and his wife to the front door which required a special key. We walked outside as if nothing had taken place.

The air felt eerie. It was too good to be true. I never took my eyes off the back of the warden's neck as I paced behind him. The voice in the back of my mind told me to make a run for it. In the blink of an eye, the warden turned around and grabbed my coat by the collar with both his hands and stared right into my eyes as his nose nearly touched mine. My body tensed up as my feet nearly left the ground. It was the final fear-stricken moment faced to move forward in my life.

"Don't you ever put me through this again. You hear me boy?" His voice was serious as I remembered it to be. I was given one option in that moment, no more chances. He had a tight grip on my coat as his eyes pierced through to my soul. Time stood still.

"Yes sir." A small shrinking voice spoke from my mouth. I did not sound or feel like myself.

The warden released my coat collar and patted the wrinkles off. He brushed my shoulders off and gave me a look I had never seen before; a head nod. I found what I had been looking for. Six years came down to a simple head nod. The sign of respect.

Chapter 8: Dear Mr. Warden

"Listen to the sound from deep within

It's only beginning to find release

Oh the time has come for my dreams to be heard

They will not be pushed aside and turned

Into your own, all 'cause you won't listen"

-Beyoncé *Listen* Single

Dear Mr. Jarmond,

It was systematic suffering the moment I stepped into your house in March of 2003. You had a strategic plan to break my fighting spirit, mental fortitude, and God given gifts. As a kid, I allowed you to take my peace and my love for myself, but I did not allow you to take my hope. I believe you saw the true heart of a lion in me. You left me with bruises, belt marks, and scars that reminded me that I was no good to anyone. Suffering was all I knew for so long as we adopted the code of silence in your residence.

You exploded at any given moment. The pain from the belt was hard, but the pain in my mind hit harder. I attempted to outlast the pain, as each whooping was a "forced confession." I could not watch the Netflix show "When They See Us," because it reminded me of the psychological torment of living in your house. After a forced confession, you made me apologize to the entire household. *Did I really do that?* My reality was distorted all because you lead with a controlling fearful spirit.

I virtually knew nothing about your history, your upbringings, or much else about your family. Everything was a secret; your finances, your personal life, and professional life. Did you not think I would have questions? You taught me nothing outside of submitting to your command. What message does that send to me Mr. Warden? My gift of curiosity often felt like a curse. You made me feel like cancer. I lived as a shark on land believing I was supposed to climb a tree but instead I belonged in the open waters.

You emphasized, "You put food in my stomach, clothes on my back, and a roof over my head, so my feelings were not important." Isn't that what you're supposed to do when you "love" a child? Only I was not your child, I was your pet. I fought for the scraps of garbage at the end of the night to feed myself as you spent money on designer wear. Meanwhile us foster kids wore $15 sneakers in middle school. It was not the kids at school who taught me to hate myself, it was you.

At 9-years-old, you brought Trivet and I to Staten Island Mental Health for a psychological evaluation. You specifically told us "not to say anything that went on in the house." When we arrived to talk to the white lady with glasses, she asked me questions and I answered them truthfully as Trivet stayed quiet. I was beat for "saying too much." You never mentioned what I said that upset you.

The psychiatrist scheduled weekly visits for me as I never spoke another word to her after that moment. I never told her how I felt even though I needed to. Here it is now, in this letter to you after you are dead and gone. I was sexually assaulted for two long years under your supervision warden. He molested me for the first time at 9-years-old. By that time, my words were already discredited as you called me "liar boy." The molestation turned into full assaults as JD used the power that *you* gave him to take advantage of me. The same location where you found my pocketknives when I was a teenager was the same place, I promised to stab JD if he ever took me into that closet again.

Your fearful tactics granted him permission to use my voice lessness to his advantage. You created a culture of shame and humiliation. When JD ran away from the house, you welcomed him back with open arms. You found it amusing as you sang the song "Run, run, run as fast as you can, you can't catch me, I'm the gingerbread man." I witnessed JD punching out glass windows, wrestling with police and being handcuffed for years. You told me "I brought the heat" when the heat was already in the house long before I arrived. You endorsed the violence that he displayed; you were the true coward for not putting your foot down when he disrespected your house.

How could I not "bring the heat" when the heat was all I witnessed? JD raised us foster children more than you ever did as he introduced all us boys to the gang lifestyle. You admired JD's alpha mentality since he was not a "wimp." How wrong you were since he was gay living in such a "manly" household. Parts of me died every day in that foster home, but I emerged from the dead as an adult. You clearly did not want to raise a "sissy boy," and I did not become one. I developed the alpha male mentality as you admired in the "alpha" in JD. It's a shame you died without ever knowing the truth about what went on.

As a man looking back on it, there was one thing worse than my body being assaulted. My mind was assaulted for years as us foster kids were paralyzed by fear you created in the house. My body sat caged as I sat in the pit for roughly 8,100 hours. Hours I could never get back as there are only 168 in a week. Your poverty mindset dehumanized everyone you came across. Your family's response when I finally told them about the sexual assaults made me realize how inconsiderate people can be. It took 12 years, but no one seemed to understand why it took so long. The lack of support from the adopted family broke my heart. I was looked at as the bad guy just as I was in your household. Breaking my silence erupted Pandoras' box as it tore me away from the family you adopted me into.

One person's response was "why didn't you tell someone if it happened for two years Schwartzen?"

Another said, "at least it's over, now right?"

Wrong. That is like telling a breast cancer survivor that, at least it's over with, now right? I struggled keeping healthy relationships with girls and many others close to me. I trusted no one. After no support was given, I was left to reach out to the foster children you adopted. I had a feeling Aeisha knew since she walked in on the assault as a kid. JD beat her up so often and that she had called her "crazy" and "delusional." Her words were not credible if she had said something. Fear kept her silent as it did me.

I was shocked she remembered it all since we each had our way of suppressing our torment. In your house Mr. Jarmond, it was hard to tell the difference between what I believed and what happened. Most people in the house knew of the assaults but feared the consequences if they spoke on it. Who would believe a bunch of lying kids in the foster care system right? Turned out, there were more sexual assaults going on than just mine.

The assault was only a partial consequence of cultivating a fear driven environment. The sexual assault scrapped pieces of my soul that took me 12 years to get back. You were a fear-based leader. You represent the systems that keep the creatives oppressed. Your household taught me not to trust white people or policemen. You were a bully as you attempted to oppress me from speaking my truth. Here it is warden.

You insulted my intelligence in that household. I convinced myself that the assaults did not happen. I suppressed it to where I had not even remembered until I was 23 years old. It took one of my high school mentees publicly share their sexual assaults as a child. They were the real hero as they spoke in front of all their peers as I nearly broke down crying. Then I remembered, you told me "real men don't cry!"

Here's something you did not expect me to find out. You changed my name in order to prevent my biological family from ever finding me. You collected a check on behalf of my mental instability. You filled my head with lies and illiterate phrases from an impoverished mindset. The ignorance and illiteracy I displayed was foreign to my family's bloodline. Poverty and ignorance are not in my DNA as I come from an intelligent tribe in Haiti. It was always in my blood to be better than the circumstances that were given to me. As you said Mr. Jarmond, blood is thicker than water.

"The adoption is like a marriage," you said, as if I understood the concept of marriage as a 13-year-old. You changed my social security number, my birth certificate and my identity. You might have fooled Pepe by switching his name from our father's first name, but my name is Schwartzenegger, I was named after a hero. You knew keeping my birth given name meant others might not find out where we were. You were right; they could not find me. My family's intelligence is underrated, as you could not keep me from finding them even with all the changes to my documents.

The human mind truly is a powerful tool as I healed myself from the trauma's in your house. I used my mind to survive 8,100 hours spent in the pit. My imagination carried me the entire way as I envisioned myself being free. My imagination inspired me to write, as I was creative. My creativity led to my freedom as I ran away at the opportunity, I saw fit! 12 years later, I read my writings from the pit, which included the first time I was sexually assaulted by JD when I was in the fifth grade. I thought Schwartzen Young Precil, was buried alive that day. Instead, he slept quietly as God prepared the way for him. My writings as a child were my liberation tool. As an adult, I thank my younger self.

Writing felt better than playing basketball. It's a shame black authors were not the ones driving fancy cars or had money in their pockets. Those were all dope dealers and hustlas as they provided for their families. You reminded me too often the importance of men providing for their family. Being reminded "real men don't cry," paralyzed my emotions for 12 years. Your condescending words hindered my ability to express myself within my relationships. I lived life with no remorse as I stole from innocent people. It took me 12 years to get over the fact that I robbed the science teacher. I even wrote her on Facebook and told her how sorry I was when I was 24 years old. Her response shocked me as she had already forgiven me. Why did I struggle to forgive myself Mr. Jarmond?

It was because I was unable to live the way God desired, which was to speak my truth. I was nothing but paycheck to your household, which is how you managed to keep the lights on in your house. "This is a business," you made sure I did not forget I was a commodity within foster care. We were all commodities as you used the money from foster care on vacations and clothes.

All's well that ends well Mr. Jarmond as I forgive you and God forgives me. The universal law of sowing and reaping had the last word. You raised me for six years, and the next six years you were in the hospital as a vegetable as diabetes and poor medical treatment took your precious life. Within those six years, you held my hand and thanked me for visiting. You were a prisoner in your body as I was at one point. I am sure you did not expect me to visit you so often did you. Outside of your wife, guess who came to visit you most frequently at the hospital? I will give you a hint; it wasn't Pepe whom you favored the most.

I never held the way you treated me against you as my heart changed over the years. The reason I made it into the professional league in basketball is because you believed I could not make the varsity team as a freshman. I sure proved you wrong huh "pops"? My decision to run away from your house was a game changer. I bet you thought of ways to torture me after I stole that cellphone at school. You underestimated what I could do. If you had sent me away, the checks would have stopped coming. This is where the ability to think for myself came into play. Your threats of sending me away made me see you as a bluff. I needed help, you knew that, yet you failed by missing the obvious as I caught on after a while.

You never intended to release me from the pit. You never planned to tell me the name of my father or mother. I forgive you. My loyalty to the people I trusted in the streets actually paid off as my homies that you told me to stay away from had my back. I turned every negative you threw into a positive. The bad things that happened, I managed to see them as good. I forgive you. The damage that was done to me can be looked at as unforgivable, yet I choose to forgive you.

This is a letter to you, Mr. Jarmond and to the rest of the bullies of the world. I take back what you stole from me through the power of forgiveness. The two years of sexual abuse was dim compared to the six years of psychological abuse. You stole my childhood memories. I am here to reclaim what was lost. Reclaim my will power, as that was one of my superpowers. My identity, my freedom of thought, my truth, and my choice. I take it all back from you by choosing not to live a life the way you treated me.

I choose not to have a fear-based leadership style as I teach kids the importance of expressing your emotions in a healthy manner. I teach others the importance of voicing their truth. I grew up and decided to lead with conviction without the fear of judgement. I became a prestigious athlete as you attempted to close the door on my basketball dreams in high school. I made the choice to clean up my act on my own accord. The most valued wisdom I acquired from you was who not to become.

I choose to use my story as a tool to give others permission to talk about theirs. I choose to be a victor of my past and not a victim. I choose to see the beautiful truth in the horrible pain I endured. The early obstacles life threw at me presented the opportunity to be the best version of myself later. The seed of truth had to die first before it can blossom into its fullness God can use later.

The hardest part of the process was changing the way I viewed my situation. It took me over a decade, but I finally let go of my pain and freed myself. As someone who went into the social work field, it is far too common the grudges people hold onto only hurt the person holding the grudge. It is easy to devalue other people when you fail to see the value within yourself. It is easy to lie over and wallow in self-pity rather than take responsibility for your situation. It is easy to crawl under a rock and blame the world for the loveless life we were given. It is easy to drift along and forget the terrible events that happened within our past. I learned that the past can come back to haunt you even when you try to forget it.

The question found I struggled with for most of my life was "Who am I?" I am Schwartzenegger Young Precil, a child of God. It does not matter how you viewed me. What matters is how I view myself. I am a child of God that held onto hope to find my family. My hope transitioned into action as I responded to my ability as a rebellious teenager.

It was God's grace that gave me a second chance not yours Mr. Jarmond. God used my pain to show His purpose for my traumatic circumstances. 13 years in foster care, six years in your house, three years in the pit and two years of sexual assault lead to one moment of liberation. My choice to run away put me in position to receive God's grace. That act of grace proved to be more effective than all the whooping you managed to give me over the years.

At 14-years-old, I held onto the Jarmond name with pride and integrity. I wore your name with excellence and did great things honoring your last name. It took me ten years to find my real family, my real father and my real last name, Precil. Now, I give the Jarmond name back to you. At 14-years old, God gave me a second chance. At 24-years-old, I give myself a second chance.

I forgive myself and give myself permission to move on. My transgressions are no longer counted against me. I witnessed the ultimate act of mercy, love. Love from a God I prayed to in the hopeless moments. The moments I thought to end my life lead me to a gracious Father showing His love in a courtroom to release me from my guilt and shame. I pray you met God while lying in that hospital bed for six years because that moment in the courtroom in March of 2009 was nothing short of God's love. In the end, I discovered my truth my way.

-From Schwartzenegger Young Precil

Mercy triumphs Justice

Through the many church services, I attended and messages I listened to about what the preacher called "Grace," never did it apply to me in practical terms. God's word never penetrated my heart since my mind was closed to receive the powerful message. However, in March of 2009, I knew exactly what "Grace" was. It's the story of how Christ loved his people. The bible is full of social rejects and people who felt like they messed up in their life. Christ loved them through their mistakes. Grace was irrelevant to my behavior. The gospel is all about unholy, unrighteous, and unjust people who followed Christ during his ministry.

There's a story in the gospel of Matthew within the Bible that talked about a man named Barabbas who was a notorious murderer. Barabbas was on trial with a man named Jesus, who was blameless of any wrongdoing, yet the crowd wanted him crucified. The crowd was asked which one would they have released Barabbas and Jesus? The crowd answered "Barabbas! Release Barabbas, crucify Jesus!" (Matthew 27:17-26)

Barabbas was released immediately, and Jesus was crucified. That courtroom moment in March of 2009, I was Barabbas, someone deserving of punishment based on the crimes I committed. I believe Jesus took the punishment I deserve when He used the warden to set me free. The Bible does not mention what happened to Barabbas after his release, if he went back to murdering people or if he changed his ways. Whatever he chose, he was free to do so because of Jesus. The love of Christ set a man, deserving of punishment, free.

***

I pictured that day in March of 2009 having a thousand different outcomes than the one that took place. I was unable to fathom the power I acquired when I ran away at 14-years-old. In the prologue of this book, I asked the question, "what if the hope in which we seek never comes?" The answer was revealed on that day, I decided to free myself from my oppressor like the slaves freed themselves in early American history. Running away is what set me free.

I still did not see myself as a hero until I shared my story at a diversion program. I knew I had a gift that had to be unleashed. I write this story for those who struggle or have struggled with anger, frustration, doubt, hardship, pain, sexual assault, opposition, death of a loved one, debt, overdue bills, or any other traumatic events that they have never seemed to get over. I share this message with you, the reader. Healing can be done. Healing will be done. The same way our relationships and life circumstances change us, is the same way we must change our negative view of opposition. It gives opportunity to become your best self.

One of the worst things people go through is rape, molestation, or being taken advantage of without the knowledge of being controlled. As a child, you do not know any better, the world is still revealing itself to you. There are far too many people that have allowed their trauma from childhood to affect their adult years. Now is the time to heal. Now is the time to forgive yourself and the oppressor as many of our ancestors.

My sexual assault came at a high price only for me to see the value in being more than a survivalist. I am a hero. A hero is not afraid to talk about their past. A hero does not shy away from the tough questions. A hero understands everyone's understandings will vary. Heroes feel misplaced at times, as they too want to feel included. A hero's gifts may be used in the wrong setting, which may be viewed as burdensome.

Heroes meet people where they are. They listen to the call to action. I am not talking about superheroes; I am talking about everyday heroes such as fireman, policeman, our veterans and soldiers, activists and people who risk their lives every day. Heroes that did not give up in their fight with cancer or other illnesses they might have had. Heroes like Tarana Burke, founder of the #MeTooMovement who risked her livelihood to speak her truth. Not all heroes wear capes and can dodge bullets. Some are hidden in plain sight with a plan to answer their calling as a leader within their generation.

Being how heavy that chapter was, I give you, the reader, to take a chance to write down some unresolved trauma. Not for others, but for yourself. One of the hardest things to do in life is to forgive the unforgivable. I did not want to expose my trauma in this book, but I understand the pain served a purpose for others to heal, not just myself. It starts with expressing the grief and pain. Trauma affects people of all ages. Do not become the supervillain like I once was. Do not use your abilities for evil. No matter who you are, you are still special. You are a child of God. Free yourself. Be Your Own Hero.

Book 2: Turning Obstacles in Opportunities

The Rose That Grew from The Concrete

Did you hear about the rose that

grew from a crack in the concrete?

Proving nature's law is wrong it

learned to walk without having feet.

Funny it seems, but by keeping its dreams,

it learned to breathe fresh air.

Long live the rose that grew from concrete

when no one else ever cared.

-Tupac Shakur

Chapter 9: Trust the Process

How do you approach life when you are given a second chance? I dedicated my high school years to redeeming myself to be my own person. I accepted that mommy or daddy was not going to come to my aid. I had to rescue myself. No one held my hand as a child, so as a teen, I did not expect things to change. I was my own person with my own flaws I dealt with them as best as I could. I had to step up and chase what I believed to be my dream, basketball. Basketball was the platform God allowed me to use to regain my voice. During the process I established principles that erupted the sleeping lion within my heart.

But we have this treasure in jars of clay to show that this all-surpassing power is from God and not from us. We are hard pressed on every side, but not crushed; perplexed, but not in despair; persecuted, but not abandoned; struck down, but not destroyed.

2 Corinthians 4:7-9

Principle 1: The vision

I finished my one-year probation term as I slowly drifted away from the street life. The streets were within walking distance, there was no need to miss it. All I knew was my experience in life up until that point. Basketball helped me remain focused on my dreams of becoming a professional basketball player. Unlearning my habits from the streets was no easy process. Like all successful journeys, it started with a vision. I saw myself as a basketball player, but I also felt the need to express myself creatively through dancing.

Having a second chance in the same environment was tough but my mental fortitude was tougher. Changing the view of myself changed how I saw everything around me. There were no healthy alternatives or constructive activities at home or in the neighborhood. I stayed out of the house by connecting with some of my boys in a dance. I set out to explore New York City and all it had to offer. If you can see yourself doing something, best believe it can be done.

A portion of my basketball vision was to start an annual student vs. faculty basketball game. I pictured myself in the locker room putting on my basketball jersey until the vision came to life. I was able to execute on the vision as a sophomore in high school. I put together the first annual student vs. faculty basketball game. I wanted to be remembered for a basketball tradition at my school. Without a precise vision, there is no way to reach a target that cannot be seen in the mind.

Principle 2: Take ownership

Back in 2009-2010, there was a dance movement on the west coast called "jerkin." Jerkin was a dance that was ignited by the New Boyz hit song "You're a Jerk." Many kids around the neighborhood danced. I like the dance and the song was catchy, so I decided to give it a try. I dedicated my time to dancing and basketball as a sophomore in college.

I no longer allowed myself to drift as I balanced basketball and dance practice. I danced across NYC and even during school hours. A girl in science class said to me, "you know what, I'm gonna call you Shwayze. You know who Patrick Swayze is?"

No. I thought, *who the heck is that?* "Oh yeah," having no idea who that guy was.

"I see you dance all the time and Patrick Swayze is a good dancer so that's what I'm going to call you." Before I knew it, everyone called me "Shwayze." I changed my entire style as I followed the trend of the time and wore bright colors and tight clothes. Shwayze stuck for a long time until I shortened it to "Shway," over the years.

My brand as a dancer erupted as my dance group performed across the city. Fame quickly followed as people around the city recognized who we were. My dance group's name was called GeekForce Entertainment (ENT). We became the top jerkin' dance group in NYC. I was part of the original four members.

My guy Mr. Fresh had the best dance moves and the freshest clothes. My guy Weirdo was a gangsta turned dancer like me. I, Shwayze, was the tallest but the fastest learner as I was new to the dance scene. The fourth member was Hollywood, I did not know him well and we did not get along. We practiced day and night. The four of us entered many dance competitions and won them all.

Many clothing companies such as National Jerk Associations (NJA), Vlados, and Neff Gear sponsored us. All sponsorships we won through competitions. Winning the NJA competition felt like winning a championship since it was nationwide. We were featured on a national poster, it felt like winning the lottery. The video had well over 50,000 views on YouTube and word spread on who GeekForce Ent was.

My dance life was kept secret from the warden's wife until one of my foster siblings told her I danced. Travelling throughout New York City with my crew was not something she was supportive with, so I went behind her back for months. The day the warden's wife saw me on YouTube I saw myself dancing online for the first time.

I danced for creative expression instead of viewership. Our rise to fame started with a video filmed in Central Park. From there, GeekForce ENT hosted our own dancing functions and photoshoots across the city. We met celebrities in the dance world such as Ben-J, Legacy, and the Bronx's very own "dance hero," Kid the Wiz. Kid the Wiz, he went on to compete in Season 8 of America's Got Talent. While Geekforce ENT was at the top dance crew, Kid the Wiz remained my competition.

After being in the spotlight for a strong year, I left the crew but kept my reputation as a great dancer for the years to come. I drifted from dancing and focused on keeping money in my pocket. I took ownership of my clothes, phone bill, and basketball fees as I took a full-time job. No one supported my financial stress, so I supported myself. Still to this day people still see my reputation from my dancing days as "Shwayze the jerk."

Principle 3: Be Coachable

My passion for basketball was not enough to keep a position on the high school varsity basketball team. I needed serious discipline. I had the skill set of a great ball player but as a sophomore in high school, I needed to mature as a student-athlete. My transition to a veteran high school basketball player came with its personal obstacles within the process. Being serious about basketball at a late age placed me at a disadvantage. My high school coach, Coach E, was the right man to help me stay diligent. His constructive criticism did not fall on deaf ears as I applied every word, he said to my game play.

"Basketball is a privilege not a right." Coach E set his expectations from the moment I put on a varsity uniform as a sophomore. His leadership paved a new way of thinking. If I arrived to practice late, I ran sprints. If I messed up in school, I was suspended from games. I monitored my behavior on and off the court by focusing on the details in my life.

I became time conscious in high school as I balanced more than the average student. Between school, basketball practice, responsibilities at home and a full-time job, left me very little time to act impulsively. I was coachable because I listened, which made me speed up the process of being a great basketball player.

Principle 4: Lead by Example

As the oldest Gaynor Mccown Varsity player, Coach E expected me to model myself as the great example. He demanded great leadership from me held me to a higher standard. I was challenged to play positions on the court I was uncomfortable with. No matter where I was placed on the court, I gave the game my best effort.

My junior season as a varsity player, I was the 7th player in rotation of a 15-man roster. Not being a starter as a junior place a chip on my shoulder as I set out to prove my worth on the team. Junior year, I lead my varsity team in bench scoring. I became a starting guard as a senior. Other players desired the starting position, but my work ethic made me standout among standouts. Coaches recognize the hard workers just as much as the talented athletes.

Most high school varsity players are talented, but they allow their talent to dictate their attitude. A player's attitude is both their biggest asset and liability depending on how it is used. Talented players do not think they need coaching since they rely on their ability. Most guys on my team possessed above average skills. I had an average skill set but my above average will power was my competitive advantage. I knew I needed coaching; I went to seek advice from coach every chance I had in order to improve my game.

Principle 5: Perfect your Craft

Do you see a man who excels in his work? He will stand before kings; He will not stand before unknown men. Proverbs 22:29 (NKJV)

Even though Abdul and I bumped heads as kids, we grew a mutual respect as teens. We woke up at 5 a.m. every weekday before school. By 5:30 a.m., we were out of the house, by 6:15 a.m., two hours before class started, we were on the basketball courts. Abdul did not enjoy basketball, yet he woke up to rebound for me as I put up hundreds of shots every morning. Not to mention the hundreds of hours at the neighborhood park with my good friend Meech. Meech knew basketball down to a science.

My offensive skill set dramatically improved as I played in spring leagues like the Jewish Community Center (JCC) and Police Athletic League (PAL). I adapted to basketball styles that differed between the suburban and inner-city communities. Not having a personal trainer did not stop me from reaching my potential of being the best I can be. By the time I was a senior varsity player, I had played all over New York City and won championships on my travel teams.

Staten Island's Gerard Carter Center had recently opened in the Stapleton community when I was in high school. Coach E hosted a few invitational training sessions with some professional basketball players. I soaked up every drill they put me through. I held myself to a different standard as an undersized basketball player. I relied on my ability to work on my craft to be a great basketball player.

Principle 6: Set the Goal

I knew very little about goal setting in high school. Playing varsity basketball for three years was pivotal to my academic achievements. The coaches ensured we took every game seriously. By my senior year, we went to the New York City PSAL A playoffs for the first time in program history. New York City playoffs are a big deal for high school basketball. We went on a strong playoff run until finally losing to the second highest ranked team in the city in the elite eight.

Most players have the desire to be "the man" in high school. They are usually very selfish. Their goal is to get their numbers as they disregard team efforts. My goal was for the greater good of the team. I showed my capabilities without forcing the issue of scoring. As a senior varsity captain, I was 5th on the team in scoring yet I was one of the only players in school history to play in college and get paid to play as a professional athlete. My senior year had the roster of three of the top ten all-time leading scorers. We set the school record of 17-10 and going the farthest in the playoffs in the schools 15-year playing history.

Principle 7: Brush the loses off

"Success is going from failure to failure without losing your enthusiasm."

-Winston Churchill

I was the athlete that looked to improve at any moment. During my three years on varsity, I lost many games and had many scoreless nights. Some of my performances were not great but I never considered myself to be a "loser," even when we lost by 40 points. Losing game, receiving bad grades, or failing at something does not make things bad. I looked at it as there being much room for improvement. As an athlete, there was no room for feeling sorry for myself, I had a goal to become a starter, play in college, and become a professional.

People have a strong tendency to give up on themselves if they did not receive their intended outcome. Losing during the process towards your goal does not make you a loser. Please reread the previous sentence. It makes you human. Failure is part of the process of success. I developed the habit of brushing off the losses I had as an athlete. The best thing I did was reaffirm myself after every bad game. I told myself "I will do better next time. I will go harder in practice." Remain focused on the bigger picture is a technique I developed to stay motivated. Challenge yourself to look beyond your disappointment in order to move forward.

Principle 8: Failure will always be there

Most of basketball players from Staten Island (or any part of NYC) face daily temptation of the street life. We all had this dream of "making it out." Very few do. We were all a step away from jail or being killed. People like Holy Moe from Park Hill did their best to use basketball as a tool to spread awareness for street violence. Like most urban communities, talent lurked in every neighborhood. Everyone played high school basketball, some played college basketball, and very few made it to the professionals. Holy Moe is a hero that made it as a professional athlete then returned to his neighborhood to show us younger ball players we too can "make it out."

The unfortunate reality is that many ball players do not "make it out." Some are arrested after their failed dream as they returned to the street life. For some athletes our entire existence surrounds our sport, take it away, and what are you left with? Whether or not you "make it out" of your situation, the corner, the violence, the block, the scamming will always be there. It does not take much effort to be in the streets. Chasing the dream is a process that has proven to be faithful to those who truly want better for themselves.

"Failure belongs to those who neglect to see the reward within the process."

-Schwartzen Precil

Principle 9: What's your "Why?"

Other than the enjoyment, being the best player at my school, and an outlet from the streets, I did not have a reason to play basketball. I met great people through basketball who challenged me in uncomfortable ways. My good friend Dougie Fresh was one of the funniest kids in the school. On the court, we were sworn enemies. If I was the best basketball player at my school, he was the second best. Dougie Fresh had high integrity but never joined the varsity team. He did not have a strong reason. Truth be told, neither did I.

I had a goal, but the goal was to be a professional. It had no intrinsic value. It was not until I stepped on the court against my classmate who was a world class boxing champion, "Skip." Skip won the golden gloves as a sophomore in high school. I attended many of his boxing matches and he did not lose a single fight. After one of his boxing matches, I asked him a question.

"How do you maintain such high intensity every match Skip?" He smiled as if he had waited to be asked that question his entire life.

"Shwayze, boxing is an art, not a sport. As an artist, my creativity is heightened when I'm punching the bag at training sessions. Boxing is nothing compared to the war I was in as a boy in Africa. Fighting for a title in America comes easy when I know I had to fight for my life in my home country. In the ring, I fight for my life not for a title."

Skip was only 15 years old when he told me about his story. From that point on I competed against him in every sport and he fueled my competitive nature. No one was more competitive than he was. When we competed in basketball, I played as if my life was on the line. God took Skip home in September 2014, at the age of 21. He had the heart of the late great Muhammad Ali. That's who Skip reminded me of as he was one of Park Hill's (Neighborhood in Staten Island) heroes. He was certainly mine as I dedicated the first European basketball game to Idrissa "Skip" Kamara.

Principle 10: Abandon the Excuses

"Behind your feelings there is nothing, but behind every principle is a promise."

-Dr. Eric Douglas Thomas

I was not held accountable in the classroom by my peers, instead, they held me accountable on the court. My good friend Billy Dukes was in my ear reminding me that "I'm making excuses when I justify a bad play or game. No one wants to hear your excuses Shwayze!" Being an undersized guard at an unknown basketball school while trying to make history did seem far-fetched. When I noticed people say I can never be a college player, I set out to prove them otherwise.

I was used to naysayers in high school as I pursued my dream. Often other people quit in the process of dream chasing and they were convinced it could not be done. They attempted to impose their negative energy on you. From teammates, to coaches, to my closest friends, I was told I could not play in college, let alone be a professional, I was only 5'10 145 lbs as a high school senior.

For everyone dream chaser there are ten dream killers. Some are peers, others are school officials, and some are family members.

"Schwartz, what are you going to do if basketball doesn't work out?" The possibility had never crossed my mind. As a dream chaser, I learned that most adults were stuck living on their "plan b."

I asked one teacher "why do you ask me about plan b?"

"I once had a dream," they told me. "It did not work out and it broke me. It is best if I would have never had the dream. Basketball might not work out the way you think it will."

The truth is I had no other vision for my life outside of a basketball player. It worked out for me. Basketball was the gift I cultivated most in high school. Teachers planted seeds of hopelessness in the students as it is common for high school students not to know what they want to do after they graduate.

"Shoot for the moon, even if you miss, you'll land among the stars."

-Norman Vincent Peale

One of my good friends, who was known as "Quote" in high school used to play basketball as a freshman. He was 6 '3, wore glasses and jumped pretty high, only he loved to sing. He was the black Zac Efron. His voice was that of an old school R&B artist. I thought of him to become the next Ne-Yo or Wale since he had great word play as he spoke with strong emotions. He drew attention when he sung, girls complimented him, and he even had a music note as his first tattoo. I think of him as the greatest R&B artist that never was. *Why?* When I asked him, he had a million reasons as to why he never pursued it.

Seeing why he never used his gift to its full capacity made me believe the fear of success stopped him. I believed those around him discouraged him not to pursue it. Sometimes, our gifts expose the hidden jealousy within others. Jealousy can blossom or plant seeds of fear in our minds that keep us from the possibility of success. It is a natural tendency to tell ourselves reasons we "can't."

When my friends from high school and I met up after we graduated, we used to complain about how crappy our high school was. We complained about our high school not preparing us for academic excellence. Being we were the first graduating class made us believe we were the guinea pigs. We always complained about the school not preparing us for the academic success in college or success in the real world. It was the same way I blamed the warden for treating me the way he did. We all have excuses.

When I reflected on who I graduated high school with I thought about the salutatorian and valedictorian in the class of 2012. One was a black male, the other a black female. Both gave speeches at our high school graduation; both attended the same middle school as I did. The female student actually grew up two blocks away from me and had African parents. The male student had African parents as well, yet they both went to highly prestigious universities after graduating from high school. Either African parents did an excellent job raising academic standards, or I made an excuse for myself.

The male went to Princeton University. *Why is it that he went to Princeton University as a black male that came from the same academic background as me but went to a highly reputable college?* He was voted most likely to succeed; I was voted greatest athlete. Our challenges might have been different growing up as he had both parents in his life. This might be true, but I still managed to go to college without my parents. When I realized that he made it from Gaynor Mccown to Princeton, I concluded that there was no reason for me not to obtain my dreams. There were no more excuses.

I told myself the wrong narrative and made excuses. I told myself "college was not for me, but basketball was." I was not educated on the academics of college, but I knew all about the basketball recruitment process. I made excuses to my academics. Most students do. We blame the teacher, blame parents, siblings, blame outside circumstances, blame our backgrounds. An immature mindset makes us neglect our responsibilities. We are programmed to put the blame on other people because looking in the mirror is a hard reality check.

In high school, I did not make excuses as to why I could not go to a Division I school. Plain and simple, I did not have the stats. That did not stop me from pursuing my dreams of being a professional basketball player. I did make excuses when I went to college as to why I struggled. I pursued my dreams of one day being a professional, I did everything I needed in order to play college basketball.

***

I had the confidence, I was competitive, but it was time to get creative. I contacted coaches and reached out to college programs who all wanted to know my academic scores. I took my SAT and scored below a 1300. The maximum score was a 2400. My college basketball programs were limited. I was creative with my recruitment and contacted the National Collegiate Sports Association (NCSA).

After I sent game film, they put together my recruiting profile and I submitted a scholarship application. It did not take long for coaches to reach out to me. The NCSA contacted my coach and I applied for a leadership scholarship award. The process was a long one, but I eventually earned a scholarship and went off to college. I wish the story could have ended there but unfortunately life has thrown me many more obstacles. My biggest one was of course dealing with relationships. My demons from my past could not be taken away through the game of basketball.

Chapter 10: Lucy's Dance

As a teenager, I reinvented myself from a street kid to a basketball star and creative dancer. I was a star athlete, dated cheerleaders, and stuck to the status quo yet I desired a committed relationship. I thought my life was like a movie where I was going to meet "the one" in high school and live happily ever after. The problem was the traumas of my past were fresh and it prevented me from opening emotionally. I was afraid of judgement, so I stuck to what I knew was emotionally safe. I had to learn the girls I attracted reflected my past of dysfunction, lies, deceit, manipulation, etc.

One of my good friends spoke to me about a problem within his relationship with a girl who had a traumatic past. My friend and I had similar upbringings as he too was a sexual assault survivor. Watching him navigate his relationship, gave me an idea of how giving loyalty to the wrong person can be very costly. His girl's name was Lucy and I was in for a big surprise when he told me about the flurry of experiences within their relationship.

My boy always had trouble building an emotional bond with Lucy since he too grew up in a broken home. He was a Christian and he explained how God gave him signs on why he should not be with Lucy. My friend chased the feeling of belonging for decades attempting to fit in with people he did not belong with. One of those people were Lucy. He did not have much going on for himself outside of soccer. It took him years to get over Lucy, but it finally ended after he had lost his entire livelihood.

My good friend's name was David. He was 6'0, brown skinned and spoke to everyone in school and was charismatic. The way he and Lucy met was by accident, like a good romance comedy movie on the Hallmark channel. He came to school to practice soccer as usual but took a later bus time and saw the prettiest girl he had ever laid eyes on, Lucy. He noticed her wearing these stylish color-coded long socks, a pair of converses, and a skirt as she stood by herself with her headphones in her ears. He had to approach her since she was his type. Lucy's skin complexion reflected that of Gabrielle Union which complimented her eyelashes, mascara and straight hair.

If you knew David, you know he always went after he wanted. He approached her as they left the bus and noticed her cute shiny braces. The school was a solid six minutes away from the bus stop, he knew that was plenty of time.

"Hi," he said, "don't I see you in school with ya girl Katie?"

"Yeah, I see you too with ya lil friends," she brushed off as they walked together.

"Well I just wanted to take the time to introduce myself." He reached out his hand for a handshake as this made her laugh at such a corny gesture. David was awkward yet determined. He went on to invite Lucy to one of his soccer games the following week. She was impressed by his skills and the two started dating. He spoke about her all the time as he and Lucy shared the same desire to escape from the realities of life. They wanted to run away together, except Lucy had her whole life planned for herself but David's only ambition was soccer.

As he spoke to me about his adventures with Lucy, I had trouble choosing which one of Aeishas' friends I liked most. Aeisha had friends that had dynamic personalities and were very attractive. Even though none of them went to my school I still made time to see them on top of my responsibilities. David began to tell me about his trouble in paradise four months into the relationship. He and Lucy broke up and he found himself in the situationship he called "Lucy's dance."

After David and Lucy broke up, he broke down in every way possible. He kept saying how she was "the one," when I told him she was not. David explained how they shared a memorable kiss and every day they spent together was a dream come true. He was blinded by Lucy and her dance. Even though she was black and had great aspirations, her father was white, and he was the decision maker for Lucy. He did not want Lucy dating a "no good athletic black boy who had no father or house training." He resented his skin color and cursed the day he was born.

I tried to tell David he had more going for himself than he gave himself credit for. He was an athlete, had great friends, received good grades, and survived harsh conditions. Still, he was blinded by Lucy's dance. He called it "love," but I knew better. He mistook the infatuation for Lucy as "in love." It was part of Lucy's dance.

I encouraged him to join the track team with me to get his mind off her. He needed a distraction, but he said Lucy was his distraction, his life was terrible. He could not see past his own feelings. He was devastated at the fact that Lucy had taken his virginity and moved on so quickly. Lucy went on to carry a reputation for herself for being that she spoke to multiple guys at once, yet David still wanted to be with her.

"God loves her no matter what she does, and so do I!" David debated whenever I told him to let her go and move on. He was too caught up in Lucy's dance. I felt bad, but at the same time I could only tell him so much.

He and I ran on the track team together as we ran our first track meet at Van Cortlandt Park. Five minutes into the race an encouraging voice spoke.

"Go Schwartz! You got a couple more miles until you hit the home stretch, that's when you push all the way!" Coach Lee, the track coach, words gave me an extra push.

His words boosted my effort. About two miles into the race, my adrenaline could not hide the pain and fatigue in my legs. I talked to myself as if I was in a video game. Every muscle in my body was sore. I saw that finish line and erupted with energy. I was possessed with the passion to win. Coach Lee greeted me with excitement as he informed me that I had the fastest time on the entire team. I tried to celebrate with David but even after the race all he brought up was Lucy and how he missed her.

His mind being so caught up on this girl raised concerns for me, so I sat him down.

"What is it about her son?"

David started, "All my life I thought I was happy without a girl or other people around me. Having Lucy as my girl makes me happy. I did not know what happiness was until I met Lucy. Now it feels like I cannot do anything without thinking about her. I do not know what to do Shwayze." His emotions blinded him from the logical decisions. He said it was more painful to live without her presence than having her around and hurting him. Lucy distracted him from life. *Was his life really that bad?* I thought.

"Distractions can be fatal."

-Schwartzen Precil

Urban dictionary defines a situationship as a "relationship that has no label on it… like a friendship but more than a friendship but not quite a relationship."

David and Lucy eventually got back together, and he seemed happier than ever. Only they did not have titles within their "situationship," so Lucy was seeing other guys. David turned a blind eye to it. The situationship worsened as the two were no longer an item but still had feelings for each other.

When the emotions are official, but the title is not it leaves much room for gray area. He loved her connection but started to slowly pull away as Lucy had been with her girlfriend's best friend and several of his close friends. It made David see Lucy in her true character.

It was a wakeup call he needed. As he moved on to another girl, Lucy decided to fight her one day after school. Lucy dragged the girl across the parking lot and as her friends recorded the entire fight. After that, no girl wanted to talk with David. Lucy made an example of what happens when you talk to her ex. Lucy instilled fear and she planned to keep David around. I felt bad, I did not know what to say or do.

He blamed himself for the relationship going bad. He kept reminding himself that he was no good at anything except soccer. He wanted to end his life early in his teenage years. It was hard to talk to him as fear had already made a home in his mind.

The people closest to David that told him that he needed to marry Lucy. Those people were just as ignorant to what went on. He looked at his skin color as a liability because he did not like the family he was born into. I told him to get use to the stereotypical comments as a black man and just prove others wrong. He was the opposite. He could not ignore the comments. He took the anger out on Lucy's dad and decided to send explicit photos to her father to get revenge. Lucy's dad showed up at his door so fast I did not get to his house on time before they started brawling.

Lucy liked David's revenge tactic and told him "two can play that game." She took revenge by confessing she had lost her virginity years prior to meeting David. He justified her behavior because of her father's alcohol addiction and domestic violence. David could not take the pain of her situation as he convinced himself that he was the one to rescue Lucy from her terrible situation. He was caught up in Lucy's dance.

"I believed I was supposed to rescue her," David said. "You know, like be her knight in shining armor and all like the movies Shway."

"Bro, how are you supposed to take her away from her pain when you have your own pain you're dealing with?" I stated. "You're ignoring the obvious son, and that's gonna come back to bite you. You're 17, how you expect to take care of her when you must build a life for yourself first? Or did you forget you have trauma too?"

"Yeah but God tells us to serve others, and I need to serve my future wife while I still can. I do not know if I'll get the chance tomorrow."

He continued to seek the thrill of being in Lucy's dance. They took photos together and posted them on social media. Everyone thought they were cute, but most people knew their business around the city. It was dysfunctional. He told me stories of how he went to Lucy's house and hide underneath beds and closets. He had to jump out of the back door, run from her dogs, and hop over fences.

"Track practice and soccer paid off huh?" I jokingly said. I went on to do some research about the "false love" we mistook for true love known as "Lucy's dance." The Greeks called it "Eros," who was the god of sexual love and beauty. I grew up calling it "cupid's choke-hold," but we referred to it as Lucy's dance.

Their actions displayed the lack of respect as they exploited each other's lusty feelings. They did not know better, but someone had to talk to him. I tried to be there for David, but my words fell on deaf ears. He was determined to do what he wanted. They entertained other people as they entertained each other. He believed he could revive the substance they had years prior, but Lucy's dance had its own rhythm and he was dancing to the beat.

Even though we drank and occasionally smoked, his drug of choice was her body. The only connection was erotic as they no longer thought about the consequences. As teenagers, they were "reckless lovers." No matter the trouble they went through they managed to see each other. It was a beautiful type of pain. One where the thirst of lust ignited their reason to be alive. If they had a soundtrack for our situation it would be "Love the Way You Lie" by Eminem and Rihanna.

"...High off her love drunk from my hate, it's like im huffin paint and I love it, the more I suffer. I suffocate..."

-Eminem

Truth be told, the girls I hung around all wanted to go to college. If I was to be successful in my relationships, I knew college was part of that solution. I did not consider myself "smart enough" for college but through my work ethic, I began to consider academic interests. It was not until the girls I was attracted to spoke about college all the time. Most of my lady friends supported me when things went wrong with my high school sweetheart.

My senior year opening night for basketball had a packed crowd of nearly 1,000 people. My friends greeted me in the facility as I looked for my girl who was nowhere in sight. Out of the 1,000 people in the crowd, my mind focused on her. We won the game and started the season with eight straight wins. We finally lost to a team we did not take seriously. My team lost momentum headed into the biggest game of the year against the Curtis Warriors.

A day before we played Curtis high school, my girl and I had a major disagreement which threw off my focus. That same day, David and Lucy had been suspended for hooking up in the locker room. This all took place the night of the biggest game of the year. To give context, for Staten Island high school basketball playing at Curtis Warriors home gym two days before Christmas was like Christmas at Madison Square garden. Electricity flowed in the facility as they were a top New York City program with a rich history in basketball.

All the drama triggered my emotions which lead me to act impulsively. My attitude showed to school officials, who told my coach, that led to a one game suspension. I was a wreck as my team competed without me. My poor emotional control bled into the next game against the second-best team. Coach E gave me the assignment for game. It was to defend MSIT high school's all-time leading scorer. He was a versatile player. I had my only scoreless game of the season. This player was known for his deadly step back, which he used during the final seven seconds in the game. His step back sealed the game as we lost by three points.

It was obvious my head was not in the game. Coach E took notice.

"Let this loss serve as a lesson. One of the reasons you're a captain is because you've learned to get through mental barriers. This is one of those barriers Schwartz. We play this team again next week and I need you focused." Tears rolled down my face as I let myself down. Fear punished me for my mistakes. I felt out of character and acted out of it. I got high and drunk later that week. I felt done with the world. One simple mistake and I threw a pity party. It was tough not seeing the bad within myself when it was what I was conditioned to see.

Determined Spirit

The following week, we played the same team. Coach decided to take me out of the game for a longer than usual amount of time. We went up 20 points by halftime without me.

"As long as we don't shoot three's early in the shot clock, we should be able to walk out of here with the win." Coach Palma explained.

I listened to the game plan but was not mentally prepared to get back in the game. I decided to listen to my gut instinct as I felt my emotions rise up. I made an instinctive leadership decision that I believe changed the trajectory of the game. I pulled Coach E and Coach Palma aside just before the start of the second half.

"Coach I want Bush to start the second half of the game."

"What are you talkin' about Schwartz? You'll be starting the second half as usual." Coach Palma said as he started to walk away.

"No coach." He turned his head towards me. "Bush had a great first half, I think we need to continue to go to him for offense." Coach E and Coach Palma look at each other.

"Schwartz, we are not changing the lineup now go warm up." His voice stern.

"This is a captain's decision. Bush will start the half off and I'll come off the bench." The tone in my voice showed that my mind was made up. Coach E and Coach Palma looked at me with a blank stare until Coach Palma finally said "ok, Bush will start, now go warm up."

The game started as Bush was in the starting lineup. Within a matter of eight minutes the other team erased a 20-point lead and cuts it to 12 by the end of the third quarter. Coach made no substitutions the entire third quarter.

Midway through the fourth quarter, the other team had momentum and cut the lead to one. Then with two minutes left in the game, the crowd erupted in praise as they went up one point. Coach Palma called a timeout. I sat on the bench ready to check in. Coach looked right at me and said "check in."

"I got this," I muttered to myself. "It's all or nothing. I got this."

I stepped on the court and went right up to the player that hit me with a step back to play tight defense on him. With a minute left in the game my teammate hit two free throws. My opponent came down the court and scored right away. So much for defense. They went up one point with under a minute life in the game.

The ball was in my hands for a split second until I shot it from inside the three-point line. Swish. The shot made me hungry to play defense as the crowd shouted "BOO!" My opponent brought the ball up the court as I played full court defense. *I had seen this before; he does his dribble moves at the top of the key and dribbles to the wing. His famous wing step back three-point shot. Not this time!*

He made his lighting quick step back and I anticipated the shot coming. I look at the shot as it's in the air. Swish. The crowd erupted as if they won a championship. They lead by two points, 68-66 with three seconds left in the game. Coach called a timeout. I kept my head up since that was a tough shot to make. Coach created a play for our leading scorer, who had 30 points, to get a quick layup to get the game to overtime. My teammate had other plans.

With only three seconds left they double teamed our leading scorer. My teammate got the ball and threw a Hail Mary from half court. The game clock buzzer goes off. SWISH. The three pointer is good, CSIM defeated MSIT 69-68 for the first time in school history. Coach and the bench stormed the court surrounding my teammate who made the shot. It was something out of a movie, unbelievable. Our biggest win in school history. Coach Lee approached me after the game and to inform me that my shot did not go unnoticed. It was pivotal to the game.

The following week, it was time to prepare for the program's first PSAL A playoff game. Coach Palma met with the PSAL A District coaches to fight for a top 10 placement in the tournament.

"We have the first-round bye." CSIM was the number 10th seed in the New York City PSAL A Division playoffs in 2012, the final team to get a first round bye. After the first-round bye, we played the first PSAL A playoff game with home court advantage and beat Frederick Douglas Academy by 20 points.

The next game was a nail biter with a team from the heart of Brooklyn Heights called Global Studies High school. The crowd was vicious the entire game and out of the 200+ people in the gym the only white people were the coaches on our bench. Being the away team in the PSAL playoffs is a very hostile environment. Global Studies was ranked 7th in the city and their hustle showed they wanted to win that game badly. We escaped with a win by two points 58-56.

CSIM Dragons basketball program had made history once again. We were the only team outside of the top 7 that had made it to the final four PSAL A Division. There was one team left to play, last year's runner up in the championship game and the No. 2 seed in the city, Long Island City High School (LIC). Their record was 25-3 while ours were 17-9. We prepared ourselves for a game of a lifetime since LIC had home court advantage.

The game was close in score the first three quarters. When coach took me out the game with six minutes left, the game took a shift. I anticipated coach putting me back in but when he called timeout without the substitution, I knew we were going to lose the game. It was my last game as a high school varsity basketball player, and I watched my team struggle defensively in the final minutes. LIC sealed the game with some late points that we didn't match.

The crowd chanted "Nah nah nah nah, nah, nah, nah, nah, hey, hey, hey, goodbye!" until the final buzzer sounded, and the game ended 56-49. I cried badly. The frustration, the hurt, the pain. I was a wreck. Coach Palma came up to me, gave me a hug.

"I should've had you in the game for the last few minutes. I'm sorry Schwartz." Our season ended 17-10 a school record that remains unbroken till this day. A few weeks later I was selected for the annual Staten Island Warren Jaques Classic All-Star basketball game. My high school playing career was over and it was time to move forward to prepare for college basketball.

Chapter 11: God's Answer

*For I know the thoughts that I think towards you, says the Lord,
thoughts of peace and not of evil, to give you a future and a
hope.*

Jeremiah 29:11

"I'm supposed to marry Lucy!" David had lost his
marbles. "That's what I am supposed to do. Forget soccer, forget
life, I love her!" I heard him plead for weeks during our final
days in high school. I felt his pain. He did not want to be alone
as a new chapter was about to begin in our lives. I myself did not
want to go away to college, truth be told.

"Please, don't let me go away! I don't want to go away!
I want to stay here with family!" I begged and pleaded with the
warden's wife. I sat in her car crying hysterically because I
feared being forgotten. I felt betrayed as my tears did not phase
her. I sucked up my tears, got myself together and went to the
only source I had left, God.

The youth group I attended in high school was a safe
haven for young creatives. Us teens had a different ability and
displayed our voices, spoken word, instruments, and I brought
my dance group GeekForce ENT to youth night to do a dance
routine. I wish I could say I went because God did right by me,
but I cannot lie about it. I attended for the cute girls. Hanging out

with pretty girls and eating candy, I could hardly believe I was in church half the time.

The youth pastor was relatable as well. He often started his sermons off by cracking jokes. He was built like an NFL player. Young, tall, black and in his mid to late 20's. He made himself relatable by playing video games, playing movies, and gave us opportunities to act in his short films. Pastor Mecdon was one of the only positive influences in the community. Even though he was older than us youth, he spoke our language. He spoke on tough but relevant subjects. His style was not the traditional reading from the bible and listen to a service format. His creative engagement sparked the interest to possibly be a follower of Christ.

Mecdon signed me, Trivet, and a few friends up for a basketball tournament. We won the championship. Mecdon filmed each of the five games we played. We were welcomed back to the church as champions. Returning to youth group after winning the championship felt like an honor. I believed God was showing me I was able to play basketball at the collegiate level. The first time I saw myself play basketball was the video highlight tape Mecdon put together from the tournament. I believed basketball was the key to my future.

One of my first prayers as a teenager was to be a professional basketball player. I used to think reading the bible answered my prayers. The Heavenly Father's love to His children will never fade no matter the behavior they displayed. I transitioned into understanding God's love as a parental relationship rather than a supreme authority governed the world.

I attempted to transcend my past without verbally confessing my sins and asking for forgiveness. I did not have a "come to Jesus moment" as a teenager. I learned a lot in youth group, including the law of reaping and sowing, otherwise known as the universal law of karma. Memories of all the phones I stole in middle school came back to haunt me. I bought over a dozen cellphones in high school all worth nearly $100 each. I went through four Sidekicks and two Blackberry phones in one year.

I asked God to show me direction for my college situation as a senior in high school. A guy from my church asked me about my future plans. He introduced himself as Peter Sims.

Peter Sims said "I overheard you talk about a decision to go to college, is that right? Do you mind if I pray for you Schwartzen?" I obliged and he prayed for me right there on the spot. Week after week he asked me if God had given me an answer.

"Yes. I believe God wants me to go away to play college basketball." I answered

"I'll pray that God grants you favor in basketball as well," and prayed for me. He prayed for weeks. I was not anxious about the decision when we prayed as I believed something good was about to happen.

Shortly after, I attended a Christian youth retreat for a few days. During the retreat, we went to a stadium where the pastor asked a stadium of over 5,000 youth if we wanted to receive the Holy Spirit. There was beautiful music, beautiful worship, great performances and then the altar call came. I watched as teens flooded the altars with their hands up, crying, and worshiping Christ. I did not move a muscle. I was unsure of what the Holy Spirit was. I used that time to ask God to show me where He wanted me to be next year. I also prayed for Lucy and David in need of their relationship. When I returned from the retreat, David said he felt distant from Lucy.

"When you were gone Shwayze, it felt strange spending time with her. When I kissed Lucy, I felt disconnected. I even saw something evil through her eyes when I kissed her Shway. I couldn't tell anyone though because I did not know how to explain it." I did not know what to say, or how to respond to David, so I left it open ended.

As graduation neared, I spoke about the doubts I had about going away to play college basketball.

Peter smiled, "God has a plan son," he continued "if He wants you to play college basketball, He will make a way for you to play college basketball." The prayers that Mr. Sims spoke over me were one of the main reasons I held onto hope. A week before high school graduation, I received a call from an area code I did not recognize. It was a college basketball coach offering me an opportunity to play for his program at a four-year university. With graduation a week away, I told Mr. Sims.

"It was God's answer to the prayer you had been asking for." He was right. I was filled with excitement. I never saw him again after that day and six years later Peter Sims passed away. He had served his purpose as God's faithful servant. He was a prayer warrior and nothing short of a hero.

The summer before I went away to college was bittersweet. I felt liberated and free as I walked away from my toxic McDonalds job to pursue college basketball. The news spread about my college basketball aspirations as I had made the newspaper. My mind absorbed the negative comments said about me in the community. I am sure there were good things that were said but I focused on the negative. One of the most frequent sayings I heard was "I wasn't skilled enough to play college basketball." I was envied for my accomplishments as I knew people waited for me to fail.

My last day as a high school youth group member my good friend Yinka pulled me aside.

"I'm gonna to miss you bro."

I did not know how to process his words. I am sure my blank stare threw him off.

"Hey, Schwartz," one of the youth leaders spoke on the microphone. "Can you come up to the front for a moment?"

What!? I'm in trouble in church!? Moms finna whoop me! My guilty conscious kicked in.

The youth leader placed his arm around my shoulder, "As you guys probably know, Schwartzen has been with us for nearly seven years and he'll be going away to play college basketball. He will no longer be with us. We just want to say

Schwartz," he turned from speaking to the crowd to look in my eyes, "we're going to miss you buddy." The youth group gave me a round of applause. "To show you how much we're going to miss you, we want to send you away with a present." He hands me a bag full of gifts

"There's one more thing we need to do before we send you away Schwartz, and that's for everyone in here to pray for you." The youth group reached their hands towards me and proceeded to pray. It nearly brought me to tears. I felt as if I knew there was a God who saw me for who I was.

Chapter 12: College Obstacles

The average college freshman understands class attendance, study habits, and minimum GPA requirement in order to continue their studies. I was in a category of my own. I virtually knew nothing about college. I was ignorant in declaring a major and the different career fields. I only knew that I was supposed to play basketball and party like a rock star. It is exactly what happened to me as a freshman. There was no vision for me being studios. I entered college like a fish out of water.

I could not re-acclimate to my neighborhood norms after a year away at college. Sophomore year I had a wakeup call from my adopted mom as gang violence hospitalized Abdul. I reconsidered the vision of myself and decided to take classes seriously. For the first three years of college, I lacked professional etiquette. The way I talked, moved, and thought was that of my upbringing.

After nearly losing my position as a residential adviser, I knew I needed professional development. God gave me spiritual accountability partner to grow with. All semester we invested time rewiring our thoughts, beliefs, and views of ourselves. From drugs to basketball, I lost the desire to do anything except increase my spiritual discipline. I experienced the fullness of my spiritual needs. I lost many friends as people did not like the new attitude, and I separated myself from immature ways.

The call to leadership replaced my negative influence with positive ones. I became the Student Senate President, Black Student Union (BSU) President, joined the National Society of Black Engineers chapter at Michigan Tech University (MTU) and continued my position as a residential adviser while balancing athletics. My aspirations as a basketball player lead me to travel abroad and play European basketball. All my accomplishments were dim in comparison to the support I received from many people at my college over the years.

The toughest part of the college journey was the inability to express myself in a healthy manner. I had serious trauma, friends from Staten island were dying and going to jail and the warden died while I was in Europe. I was arrested on a traffic violation for being profiled as a drug dealer. Those traumas made me reassess my place in society.

It is far too common for others to allow their pain to dictate how they treat others. I refused to allow the pain I felt over the years be the reason why I hurt others. Most unaddressed traumas add to the misery of the world. As a kid, I chose to keep quiet, suffer in silence, and do what I wanted. As a young adult, there was a shift into self-liberation. I knew there was nothing that could stop me from being my own hero.

A journey of a thousand miles begins with a single step.

Chinese Proverb

I hopped on the plane for the first time and my ears popped on the ride. It was a terrible flying experience. When I landed, I was greeted by an employee from the university. I stepped off the plane and noticed the air was different. It seemed too fresh for my inner-city saturated fume-filled lungs.

"Hey there!" Welcome to da U.P!" She spoke with a high-pitched voice and an accent I was unfamiliar with. Her cheeks were puffy red, and her blonde hair was slightly messy. She continued, "your name is Schwartzen right?"

"Yeah," I answered hesitantly.

She introduced herself as she drove another student and I to the university campus housing. I couldn't help but look outside the window of the large white van we rode in. Trees, trees and more trees. My head pressed against the glass window as if I was moving to another foster home. One question pondered my mind. *Where am I?*

We approached a large brick building. *Ok, at least I know there's a train station.* When I stepped out of the van and saw it was the university's residence hall. *Not a train station.* All the parents were helping their kids get settled in. It made realize that I had always been on my own. I pulled out my Blackberry phone. No cellular service.

When I walked in the building, I was greeted by upperclassmen students that helped settle me in. They were residential advisers (RA)

"Wassup fam!?" One RA asked as he had an urban look with his basketball shorts and backwards snapback.

"What are you listening to?" He took noticed my blue and white colored headphones.

"Nas." My low toned voice took me by surprise.

"Okay! I mess with Nas fam!" He replied. "You play basketball?"

My own voice sounded foreign as my ears adjusted to his Midwest accent. "Yeah, I was recruited by Derek Gardner." I said with confidence. Next to the guy doing all the talking was a 6 '6 light skinned guy who wore tight skinny jeans and a backwards hat. *Two black guys in charge, go figure.*

"That's wassup, we're on the basketball team as well. I'm the captain, you can call me DeeBrown. We got some runs going on today if you tryna hoop."

"Bet." I went up to my room.

The room was on the second floor the first door to your left, room 212. I noticed the first thing that resembled home for me, my name tag on the room door decorated from a New York State License plate.

DeeBrown entered the room. "How do you like it so far fam?" He asked.

"It's good. Hey, can I use your phone mine doesn't work out here, and I need to call my folks." I asked.

"Sure!" He handed me his iPhone 4 and walked out of the room.

What's good with this dude? Why he was being so nice to me? Does he know I can rob this phone right now? Survival mode kicked in, but I caught myself. *I gotta call adopted moms, lemme make that call first.*

"I want to come home, I don't like it here." I spoke

The warden's wife was no help. There was no pleading with her, so I ended the conversation. I cried as I had felt the horrors of being forgotten all over again. I was dramatic since it had only been there a few short hours. Trauma can make things bigger than what they are. I cried for a good 10 minutes. No one saw me as I stayed in my room. I got myself together and left the room to return the phone to DeeBrown.

I cried because...

"Where are you?" Friends inboxed me from back at home wondering where I was. My phone had no service. All the "where are you" messages at once filled me with heavy anxiety. Most of my basketball teammates were from inner-city Detroit. Little did I know I was far from it. The lack of solitude was extremely difficult as the dorms were loud from all the excited freshmen in the new year. The tears I cried spoke "where is your God?"

I cried in my dorm room for what felt like weeks.

The recurring trauma slid down my face cheeks.

I cried because I felt like no one understood my pain.

Is basketball worth it? It's only a game.

I cried because playing basketball coped with the heavy bleeding on the inside.

My whole life I had been trained to survive, not thrive.

I felt alone all over again. *Where is my mother?*

My phone did not work, I missed my brother.

I cried because the oxygen from the trees made the air too clean.

I'm from New York, where the atmosphere is mean.

I cried because the people around town stopped to ask me "how's it goin' dere aye?"

"I want to go home; I do not want to stay!"

I cried from a strange look I gave after a friendly smile.

People wore different clothes; this place was not my style.

I cried because this was not New York City, it was not what I knew.

This was not a place I could get used to.

I was not home anymore where *"Real men don't cry."*

I always clung to my culture; I had a hard time saying goodbye.

Obstacle 1: Change

Have you ever been in a certain area your entire life then end up somewhere else so suddenly? You were never given the chance to process such a dramatic change since it happened quickly? If you have, you know what I am talking about. If not, I will draw the picture as vividly as possible.

Back in my neighborhood, basketball and football were the dominating sport cultures. In the Upper Peninsula hockey was the sport of choice. My university was in the same county as the birthplace of professional ice hockey. I knew nothing about ice hockey, yet it was the sport of choice. I could not contribute to conversation on the topic of hockey, country music, or fishing. Being a freshman in college, I found myself feeling like a fish out of water. I asked myself, can a leopard change its spots?

When I walked around the community there was no public transportation, no smell of garbage, and the only noise was that from the bird chirping outside. People spoke, walk and talked different. The food was foreign to me and I felt like an alien that had crash landed on Mars. In New York, making eye contact with someone can get you into trouble. In the U.P, eye contact and saying hello to strangers was the norm. *There is no way I will ever get used to this place* I told myself. God had other plans for me.

I stayed on campus with the other freshman recruits who were from different parts of the country. We laughed, joked around, watched videos, and acted as if we were freshmen. Some called me "Shwayze," others called me "New York." I adopted the nickname "Fabolous" (like the rapper) when I chipped front tooth my first week on campus. I ran into a glass window after I thought it was an entrance opening.

"Dude are you alright?" Asked a bystander as soon as my face hit the glass. "Hold your head back it's coming from your nose dude."

I cupped my hands over my face as I scurried over to the lobby bathroom. My teammates came in shortly after.

"Shwayze, you aight fam?" DeeBrown asked. I picked my face up from the sink and open my mouth to the horror the mirror showed as my teammates gasp.

"WHOAAA! Dawg, what happened!?" My group of teammates asked in unison.

I looked at myself in sudden terror!

"My tooth! It's gone! What happened to my face!? This ain't my face!" I yelled. My teammates stayed silent. Half my front tooth was chipped.

DeeBrown chimed in, "Well whose face is it Shwayze?"

All my teammates burst out in laughter. I laughed internally since tears came to my eyes. The joke came at the perfect time. DeeBrown knew how to make comedy out of any circumstance. He had the gift of gab. His ability to lighten everyone's mood around him was incredible.

"Can't change the world, unless we change ourselves." -
Christopher Wallace aka Biggie Smalls

Everything around me had changed yet, I did not. Instead, I coped with the change. I used drugs, alcohol and partied like the average college freshman. My circumstances were abnormal. I should have been open to the change, instead I rejected it. The lack of mental preparation for college made me focus on what I was good at, playing basketball.

I increased the number of hours in the gym. To compete in college, you need more than hustle and heart, you need elite skills. I developed my skill as a freshman. Motivated to be a starter in my first college season, I trained with the other recruits. Just like in high school, my work ethic was the key factor for separation from the seven recruits. Coach selected me to start the first game of my collegiate career against NCAA Division II Bemidji State University.

Obstacle 2: Lack of roots

My best performance as a freshman was the season opener. I led all freshmen in scoring. I made more three-point field goals in one game than I did my entire senior varsity season. Even though we lost to Bemidji State, I envisioned myself in the race for Freshman of the Year. The hype went to my head as I partied and celebrated as if I had won a national championship. My ego took over as the very next game against NCAA Division II Northern Michigan University where I had been humbled.

I did not score a single point in the 28 minutes I played. Their 5'9 point guard outperformed me with the multiple dunks he had in the game. We lost by 50 points. After that game, I lost the starting freshman guard position. My vision of winning Freshman of the Year faded. We played a tough schedule against NCAA Division II and Division III opponents. My performance fluctuated. Throughout the season as I lacked the roots needed to stay consistent.

The disappointment within myself lead for me not to talk to anyone for weeks. I did not want to publicize my struggles. I felt shame from the prodigal lifestyle I lived. I was caught up in the idea of looking like I had it all together. I felt like people expected me to fail. I did not want to give others the satisfaction of knowing my pain. The lack of being rooted in values enabled me to continue smoking and drinking. Roots are anchors to the principles and values others do not see. Since I had poor relationship etiquette, I did not seek advice from anyone. Sink or swim, it was all on me.

My freshman season could have been successful. Deciding not to reach out to those who care about you can do more harm than good. Do not make the mistake of allowing your pride to prevent you from doing the right thing. In the world we live in today, you can phone a friend, mentor, or relative for some advice. As a young athlete, I was prideful to and was unable to keep high morale throughout the semester. Lack of roots forced me to drift away from the things I valued most.

***

As a freshman, I was a member of the Black Student Union (BSU). It was a place to soak up the wisdom from mature upperclassmen. It was my first exposure to positive peer black leadership. Majority of my teammates were black, two of the six residential advisers were black, and student government officials were black, yet less than 10% of the student population at my university were black. Being at a predominantly white institution (PWI) there was no celebration on Dr. Martin Luther King Jr. Day.

I had no interest in being a leader within the organization. I was content with giving my opinion during the discussions. The number of black leaders matched the number of black inner-city underclassman. One of my favorite topics was the topic of love. I had an ignorant response to the question, "What is love?" Being young and impulsive I gave the answer that came to mind. The BSU president explained why I was both correct and incorrect about my answer to "what is love?"

Understanding the history of how the Black Student Union started at the university placed a desire in me to one day create my own legacy. I had the honor of being mentored by several of the BSU founders. Some of the members acted as "keepers of the flame" as they carried themselves as respectable black man and woman. They held us freshman to that standard, which I did not conform to. We clashed with the upperclassman as some of the underclassman wore pajamas around campus. The BSU president took it personal and fought the kid who wore pajamas around campus. He was out to prove a point.

"Know where you come from, and you'll understand where you are going."

-Schwartzen Precil

***

My background had no affiliation with young respectable black male figures. My mind was set on partying as the thought of responsibility did not attract me. I did not know what my values were. I had guidelines to my behavior. Instead, I was rooted in the New York state of mind, my culture, and the upbringing on the foster care. I learned things the hard way. Freshman year was my trial year as to what I did and did not like. I sought assistance for the financial aid process where I took out loans, got an on-campus job and used scholarship money.

I took an interest in a creative writing course. The professor was from the Bronx, New York. We were practically siblings. Dr. Loony had a chill demeanor and spoke with elegance during his lectures. When I did an assignment on Jay-Z and Kanye West's "Watch the Throne" album I felt like a scholar. Hip-hop was my language. Most of the students had never heard of the album. They were used to country music. I was the only black person (both male and female) in my class of 20 freshmen. My roots were in my culture, my culture did not acknowledge asking for help when the lack of roots occurred.

Obstacle 3: Complacency

"The tragedy of life is not found in failure but complacency. Not in you doing too much, but in doing too little. Not in you living above your means, but below your capacity. It's not failure but aiming too low, that is life's greatest tragedy."

-Benjamin E. Mayes

Complacency is the one obstacle that could have kept me down for the rest of my life. This is the obstacle that kept most people from growing up over the years. My friends were complacent after completing a year of college. I did not blame them since I was content after my first year as well. We shared our college experience with one another then I realized their experience was completely different than mine. I asked myself *why*.

I went away to college while they attended local community colleges. I focused on sports in college, their focus was class. I was involved in student orgs on campus, they were not involved in any extracurricular activities. They were content with their first year of college, I felt like I needed to go back some day. I realized I was a little different since I sought solutions to feeling lonely and depressed at college.

The level of intelligence upperclassmen like DeeBrown and BSU President Jay Moore displayed opened my mind. Their life experience made me listen to their actions more than their words. They were from Detroit and knew it's history, I knew nothing about the history I came from. They came to college to better their future, I went as a ticket out of my neighborhood. They held leadership positions as black men and understood the importance of maintaining healthy relationships. I rarely spoke with anyone in my adopted family about any of the problems I faced.

I enjoyed being a young college athlete after being held to a higher standard throughout high school. I was never lazy as I often looked for areas of growth even as a freshman. David called me daily as we shared stories of our post high school experience. His bond with Lucy was severely damaged yet he still held on. He was content with the dysfunction, but the words he shared hurt my ears. Complacency is more than the surrounding environment, but from the people within your circle. Another word for complacency is content. Being content with only being an athlete made me feel terrible. It can take a significant event to get out of the mindset of being content. Being around DeeBrown and Jonathan ensured me that I was not stuck in being satisfied with what I accomplished.

Obstacle 4: Unfamiliar territory

Being saturated in another culture while being unrooted to my own enabled me to pick up the lingo from those around me. During college breaks, I spent time with my boys, and they noticed my change in language. Adapting to the Midwest culture made me copy their mannerisms and the lingo from individuals raised in Detroit. My surrounding environment had severe effects on my emotional health.

With my schedule being different at college, I barely had time to talk with David. When he told me, Lucy began to put her hands on him I was unsure how I could help. I blamed myself for not knowing the solution to his problems. David looked to me for advice as if my words were fresh water from a wellspring. My own pain of loneliness overwhelmed my mind. I could not help him because I myself needed help. They broke up and got back together more times than I can count. Their horrible situationship was clouded by erotic lust. Their toxic mental cycle became tolerable to each other.

I had innumerable arguments with my high school sweetheart during that time. We were poison to one another but the thought of leaving her for good left me lifeless. We attempted to move on, but the seriousness of our emotional trauma prevented us from knowing how to do so. The only consistent aspect of my life was our inconsistency. The damage from the failed relationship left me at my lowest place known as rock bottom.

Obstacle 5: Rock Bottom

Then you will call to me. You will come and pray to me and I will answer you. You will seek me, and you will find me because you will seek me with all your heart.

Jeremiah 29:12-13 (NKJV)

The pain during freshman year enabled me to declare war against myself. I increased the amount of substance within my body to escape my mind. Fear spoke as clear as ever *you're being forgotten by everyone since you're not around anymore.* I went to class high or hungover several times a week as my motivation for school faded. I hustled to keep money in my pockets as all I wanted to do was distract myself from my emotional torment. *Maybe this is why I felt neglected my entire childhood. I was supposed to be forgotten by everyone in my life.*

My heart grew cold and vengeful as the world I once knew was gone. I blamed God for my circumstances. My immature mentality leads me to drift away from my established principles. I felt cheated and lifeless as my spiritual life suffered. I took my frustration out on myself with the intention to hurt God. *Life was great before college, I went to church, I had weekly haircuts, I had great income, and all my friends were supportive.* The light of hope grew dim as I lost self-respect. I could not shake the feeling of loneliness at the university I attended.

One night, after I casually smoked and took a few shots of hard liquor I walked to my dorm room. I entered the room, walked to the mirror and leaned over the sink. The reflection I saw was ugly. I was a mess. This was about the 100th time I had done this. I laughed and spoke gibberish as my drunkenness was in control. The laughter turned into weeping, which transitioned to anger and my anger manifested into suicidal thoughts.

The battle with my inner demons needed to end. It was time to check out. Mentally, I was on autopilot, each day felt like the last. Emotionally, I was numb, I forgot what it was like to enjoy life without alcohol. Spiritually, I was drained, I had not prayed or went to church all semester. I was tired of being tired. In the corner of my eye, I saw a blade on the counter. I was ready to slit my own throat and watch the blood ooze out as I imagined my spirit standing over my lifeless body. My thoughts lead to actions as I picked up the blade.

My last conscious words. "God, if you're real and you're really out there, help me because I'm done with this life!"

Immediately, my heart raced as my body felt warm. My blood circulation increased. I placed the blade back down on the counter. I was scared and I walked to my bed to lay down. Laying down, I felt a hammer continuously slamming against the left side of my chest. BANG! BANG! BANG! The pounding last about two minutes. When it stopped, I lifted my head and neck to the ceiling. The effects of being drunk and high physically left my body. I lost complete control of my body as my mind had sobered up. My head and neck were gracefully placed back on the pillow. My eyelids were heavy as I closed them. It became hard to think. *Had prayer really done this?* I do not recall how I fell asleep. but I woke up and felt lighter than ever.

Chapter 13: Dawn of a New Hero

"Home, a place where I can go, to take this off my shoulders, someone take me home."

-Machine Gun Kelly, single "Home".

When I returned to Staten Island at the end of the semester, I felt disconnected from the place I once called "home." The house was deteriorating. I no longer had a room, a bed, or any space for my presence. I had no time to be in solitude. I slept on an old leather recliner chair for seven months. Being back from college, I did not have money. Something had to change since I was back at square one. My only option was to go up. While away at college, some of my boys served time in jail, were shot, or died from gang violence. Instinctively, I wanted to go back to the street life. It felt like it was all I knew. Instead, I spent my down time on the courts of the local neighborhood.

After hustling for a couple of weeks, I took a job as a door-to-door salesman at Verizon FiOS. The first couple of weeks, I survived by collecting the base salary. My first job in the real world and I showed no effort in the position I was in. My boss was unafraid to show how he felt about slackers. He fired multiple people who were unproductive. Six weeks on the job and I did not have a single sale. My boss, Jeffe, had a sit down with me that lit a fire under me.

"Your job is in jeopardy if you don't make a sale soon." I decided to pick up my effort that week. The process of door-to-door sales cannot be cheated. It is a numbers game. The more doors I knocked on, the more people I spoke with. I learned it is better to work smarter rather than harder. After a week of maximum effort, I was left again with no sales.

"I am going to have to let you go if you cannot make a sale by the end of next week." Week seven, still no sale. I sat back in his office.

"I am doing my best Jeffe, I know I can get a sale!"

"You do not get paid based on effort, Schwartzen. I pay you to produce results. I do not care how you get the sale just do it!"

On the Friday night of week eight at 7pm, I sold a cable package and made my first sale with the company. I walked into the office Monday morning and was greeted with a round of applause. The next day, I sold two cable packages. I caught momentum and developed a method that allowed me to execute. Going from eight straight weeks of no sales to being one of the top salesmen in the entire New York City District by the fifth month was no easy task.

Speaking to people became easy to me. It was my competitive advantage as I developed speaking skills. There was an art to building rapport and overcoming objections. Discovering a customer's needs became second nature. Hearing "no" was never discouraging as it took me on average 10 "no's" to hear one "yes."

I kept track of every door I knocked on and saw the trends. For every 10 doors I knocked on, I received nine "no's" and only one "interested." That one "interested" meant that person was interested in listening to what Verizon Fios had to offer. I had a solid 90% close rate once I was able to negotiate a lower price from what they were paying. The accuracy of my initial hook broke down natural walls people instinctively have when they see a black man approaching their door. Unfortunately, due to my skin color, it did not matter what I said to certain individuals, they never bothered to listen.

The money I made at 19-years-old, was used to buy sneakers and fresh clothes. I spoiled my girl with jewelry, including a diamond ring, which she lost. I partied all over NYC but attending parties in Staten Island was never a good idea. Most of the parties ended in shootouts, fighting or police raids. I was nearly shot attempting to break up a fight between two rival gang members. Attempting to be the peacemaker in hostile environments was very unwise. After months of the same routine, I felt unfulfilled as if I was a freshman in college again.

Most of the guys I grew up around became scammers. I learned the hard way what it meant to go the legal way even when others were not going. It did not take long for me to be promoted to a team leader within the company. I felt the jealousy from the dozens of colleagues at the office. Jeffe spoke to me about a potential management program that offered a permanent management position within the company.

"I need some time to think about it." I told him.

"What's there to think about?" Jeffe asked.

"Whether or not I want to go back to college and play basketball or stay here and work." I responded.

"College? I know people in this company who went to college and never used the degree they graduated with. You're great in sales and could easily make six-figures here while you're young. Besides, you don't think you'll go to the NBA or play professionally one day, do you?"

It was as if the record table was hit as a needle in my mind went haywire. It triggered my trauma. I sat in his office and I thought about the many times I was told I could "not" do something as a child. His words reminded me of the teachers that told me to "have a plan b." At that moment an image popped in my head of me playing European basketball. It was the pinnacle that ignited my decision to leave the company.

A conversation with a former basketball teammate opened my mind. I told him my plan to attend a community college.

"Shwayze, you better off coming back here and playing here fam. You better than the community college hoopers."

Maybe I should go back. I thought. I was fearful of losing myself and everything I worked for like I did my freshman year. *Do I truly want to take the risk?* Not knowing what to do. I prayed.

"God, do you want me to go to community college or take a management position?" I did not even mention my former university. A few days later, the unthinkable happened. I walked into the YMCA to play basketball as usual and saw a familiar face in the corner of my eye. I spotted Coach E. My face lit up when I saw him.

"Schwartzen, what's going on!? What are you doing back out here? I thought you were back at college." He darted with questions.

"Man, Coach E, college was tough. It was hard being away from friends and family. The financial stress was weighing me down. I could not handle it." I responded.

His face showed discomfort. "You need to go back to college and get your education."

"I will, I was accepted into community college and thought about playing basketball there."

"No," he spat. "You need to go back to the school you were at. That is where you need to be. I saw the pictures online, that's the university you have to attend again." His words pierced my spirit. I had not seen him for several years and here he was giving me wise counsel. There was no question that God orchestrated the encounter. I emailed admissions at my former university and was enrolled in the Spring of 2014.

The following week, I sat in Jeffe's office. He started with the assumptive close. Classic technique from a true salesman. "When do you want to start the management training program with your fellow colleague?"

"Actually, I'm leaving in two weeks. I'll be heading back to school to play college basketball. I appreciate the leadership opportunity, but I have other plans." I spoke with pride and liberty. His reaction was priceless. I saw him several years later, weeks before I hopped on my flight to Europe to play basketball.

"When I pursued my education, my dream followed."

-Schwartzen Precil

As soon as I got back to campus, people noticed my level of maturity. I felt back in my element. One class enrolled in educated me on the theories of poverty within urban communities. The class piqued my curiosity as I asked the professor many questions during the class. My narrow mind was fully opened once I began reading the books that held many of the African American narratives that were not taught in school.

I became obsessed with reading about the truth on Black America. "The New Jim Crow" by Michelle Alexander was a book I decided to present on during class. Seeing the statistics of black mass incarceration in America between 1970-2010, I learned the truth about my social position in America. My mind grew in ways I never imagined. I cried not because I felt lost, but because I began to experience a rebirth. One book called "Amazing Grace by Jonathan Kozol showed information about Brooklyn, NY during the 90's. It ignited my curiosity to question my upbringing in foster care. I reached out to a foster parent thought Facebook before the semester ended.

A week before my trip to see my former foster parent, I received a 4am phone call. I was laughing and enjoying myself with my teammates in the residential hall when I received the call. My phone vibrated in my pocket. It was my adopted mom. I picked up the phone wishing I had not. I answered playfully as my teammates carried on

"Abdul is in critical condition in the hospital. He was stabbed in the streets." Her words sent a metal needle stuck right through my heart.

He's dead! It's my fault! All my anxiety alarms rang like a thief attempting to break into the White House. I hung up the phone. My face numbed as my hands began to shake. The water works flowed from my eyes. *I had lost my brother to the streets. Why God? Why now?*

***

When I returned to Staten Island, I felt the tension in the neighborhood. Word spread that I was back in town and the question was posed. "When was I going to retaliate on the guys that stabbed Abdul?" I was happy to be home, but the knowledge I acquired the previous semester heightened my consciousness. *The last thing I need to do is get caught up in the streets again.* I decided to spend my semester summer break speaking about my transition from the street life. Instead of retaliating, I spoke publicly on the importance of acquiring knowledge outside of the culture you grew up in.

"Deciding to trade street credit for college credit was a key to the change in my life."

-Schwartzen Precil

Summer 2014 was spent travelling throughout the city as there was a high demand for youth advocacy against street violence. The more I spoke up against violence, the less anxious I felt about losing my life for the cause. Fear attempted to tell me I was the next victim to the streets. My new eyes tore my mind away from the inner-city mentality. My homies around the neighborhood took notice as my reputation slowly changed.

The day I crossed paths with my brother's alleged attacker was a real awakening. I used my common sense to leave the area as I prayed asking God to forgive him. My pride and ego were unaffected as others called me "college boy." I did not seek revenge even though others said college had made me "soft."

I explored my creative gifts by co-starring in short films, participating in poetry slams, and speaking throughout the city. I fell in love with the creative arts as I indulged in reading that summer. I managed to balance the training schedule with my good friend Ant as I prepared to play my sophomore basketball season. We were in his backyard at 5am every morning chasing the one thing that kept us motivated, basketball.

A Hero's Test

"The ultimate measure of a man is not where he stands in moments of comfort and convenience, but where he stands at times of challenge and controversy."

-Dr. Martin Luther King, Jr.

Before returning to the university at the end of the summer I attended a baby shower. Little did I know I was in for an unpleasant surprise. Someone from my past who I did not get along with reminded me of how much hate I harbored in my heart. When I saw their face, it triggered the built-up anger over the years. *REVENGE!* Fear yelled.

Within that moment, I second guessed myself about not avenging Abdul. I was willing to throw away all the progress I made that entire summer. Out of nowhere, as if God himself came down from heaven an old friend approached me.

"Man, Schwartz, I'm proud of how much you've changed this summer. You matured son." He spoke as my eyes were fixed on my enemy's face. He gave me a love tap on my chest to get my attention

"Think about where you're at son. If you fight him now, it negates everything you've worked hard for. Aren't you the one that told me I need to forgive others because Jesus forgave us?" His words held me by the neck. I was choked up by his words. Forgiveness poured into my heart like a raging tsunami. Anger and revenge were evicted at that moment.

Chapter 14: Heroes Don't Choose Callings

"If you want to make the world a better place take a look at yourself and make a change."

-Michael Jackson

As a first-year residential advisor (RA), basketball, academics and the Black Student Union VP, I enhanced my time management skills. As much as I developed professionally, the inability to think for myself led to nearly losing my position as an RA.

I was off campus the night I was scheduled to be on campus. A brawl happened on campus. Blaming my peers did not stop me from nearly losing my job. My employer did not care who I blamed they only cared that I was not where I was scheduled to be. I faced a probationary period and walked on eggshells. It was the wake up I needed to remove toxic people from my circle. I dropped my "blame others" attitude and decided to take full responsibility. It started with the change in my mind.

Opportunity 1: Change

And do not be conformed to this world, but be transformed by the renewing of your mind, that you may prove what is that good and acceptable and perfect will of God.

Romans 12:2 (NKJV)

At first, I did not like the idea of change, who does? The idea of quitting was even more discomforting than change. I needed to change those who influenced me. During the process, I noticed I attracted individuals from broken backgrounds. People who grew up in hostile environments reflected a younger version of myself. I intentionally mentored them to become leaders. There was a shortage of black upperclassman during my sophomore and junior year. The inaugural football team had attracted students from the inner-city. Their mind was confined in the neighborhood they grew up in. It was as if I looked at my 18-year-old self.

I encountered many underclassmen who had a passion for sports and God. They had a difficult time adjusting to the Upper Peninsula just as I did three years prior. They coped with their pain in the same way I coped with mine. The BSU club was the only time I had time to get to know each of them. There was a shortage of upperclassmen leadership as the African American underclassmen had outnumbered the African American upperclassmen at 10 to 1.

The more I spoke at the BSU meetings, the more authentic I became. My authenticity ignited my rapport with the students. My subconscious mind shifted as I had previously limited myself to those, I shared similar backgrounds with. I went against the principles of "keep to yourself" I grew up believing. God transformed my mind in ways I did not yet understand.

I formed new beliefs about myself and others as I continued to grow in knowledge. The common factor at the university was the sudden unexpected change. I saw the possibility of being a bridge for those who were local to the area and for those who were new to the area. The solution, I used my position as an orientation leader and class seminar assistant to engage with the students who experienced major culture shock. It complimented my leadership positions as the BSU and Student Senate president.

Basketball became low on my priority list as I was no longer fixed on my cultural upbringings. My adaptability and interpersonal skills were put to great use. I did what I could to bring unity to a community that seemed to be behind in the times. The events I hosted were creative and critical to the betterment of the community.

Opportunity 2: New seeds

When I was a child, I spoke as a child, I understood as a child, I thought as a child; but when I became a man, I put away childish things.

1 Corinthians 13:11 (NKJV)

I had to see my mind as a garden that was ready to have new seeds planted within my thought process. Little did I know God had planned to use a freshman with a similar background like mine. We met during the passing of classes and we shared our experiences of growing up in the inner-city. The underlying factor was our lack of positive influence within the environment we grew up in. There was a desperate need positive leadership, so I set out to be the example on campus.

The freshman I connected with was wise beyond his years. His mature attitude was admirable. We had different friend groups but being that we were both athletes we were within the same circle of influence. We lifted weights together, I helped him with his academics, and I felt positive around him.

One day we spoke about our views about God. He and I dedicated unanticipated time to discover the truth about our broken backgrounds. After understanding our similarities, it was obvious. We were our own liberators that made the choice to call on God when we were lost. We had no fathers to guide us growing up as we were our own heroes. His name was KD, and with his help I grew my relationship with God within one semester as we journeyed to learn the truth about Christ.

Seed #1: The first seed that was planted in my restored mind and watered was accountability. When KD had presentations, I asked professors to sit in during his class hours. I assisted KD academically by tutoring him. His presence helped me to understand what it meant to be a true friend. Our sharp accountability gave birth to a new level of discipline. We kept each other encouraged when we faced distractions. He had my back, I had his.

We searched through the Bible to find solutions to our problems. We started with the book of Proverbs for wisdom. After reading Proverbs, the stories of Jesus came to life. We lost the desire to party and instead spent all hours of the night reading the Bible and listening to worship music. Many people did not like the change in attitude or behavior, I did not care. We kept each other accountable.

Seed #2: The undeveloped guidelines I missed from proper parenting created the desire to be sound in my decision making. I developed a sound mind by ignoring other people's opinion of me. I was outcasted from not smoking or drinking as a college student. It was the first time I felt in control of my thoughts and actions. I gained the ability to think for myself as I was uninfluenced by my peers.

Seed #3: The level of maturity I experienced during that phase allowed me to grow in my faith. When KD and I were around each other, our personal problems were ineffective. There was a shift in my heart as I prayed and developed an attitude of gratitude. My faith grew to a point where I believed God could truly do anything. The newfound fire I had for life was unmatched at 20-years-old. My mind opened to God's will for me. One day KD challenged me.

"Aye bro, you know I've prayed for God to wake me up without an alarm clock for like a week now. I think you should try it." KD said.

"What, you serious? Nah I'll probably miss class if I do that." I refuted.

"Do it for one night and if He does not wake you up, use the alarm tomorrow." After the first night, it changed my life forever.

Opportunity 3: Exploration

I was given a new direction as I began to develop a new motivation outside of basketball. The newness of life within the kingdom of heaven made me feel alive. Basketball became less enjoyable. I felt called to a higher purpose. One that gave me the ability to use my spiritual gifts and not my physical ones. The gift of exhortation, the gift of knowledge and the gift of prayer.

"Reinventing yourself requires an extreme amount of effort as it may go against the status quo."

-Schwartzen Precil

KD and I were treated with kindness by community members and attended a Christian retreat with a fellowship group for a week. The open waters near the beach at the retreat was an unforgettable sight. The thunder and lightning danced through the clouds as the thunder boomed through the dark sky. KD and I stood at the beach near the water staring at the visible lightning. It was a clear view of heaven.

We spent seven days in the wilderness with trees, a guitar, and a campfire. Not an environment I was used to, but I was open to the experience. One night, we listened to gospel songs played by a worship artist, who we called big David. His magnificent voice echoed a beautiful song. It was the perfect moment to close my eyes and be present. I opened my eyes and looked right in the fire and cried. The fire burned as though it represented the old my being burned away.

On the final night, KD and I took a boat ride where we looked up at the stars and gazed upon God's creation. Heaven had come down to earth. We ended the night with a final group discussion for men. As I listened to each of them speak, I learned I was one of many sexual assault victors in the room. It affected the way men viewed God. I realized I was one of many who suffered as a child. The spirit within me empowered me to talk about the history of my upbringing.

"A single act of vulnerability from someone can lead others to express their authenticity."

-Schwartzen Precil

Shortly after the retreat, I took a fellowship as an anthropologist and left the country for the first time. I spent a few nights at cottages in the countryside of Finland. I woke up to alpacas and donkeys standing on the outside of my window several feet from where I slept. In Finland, the stars seemed endless. Summertime in Finland meant white night, where the sun never fully set. One night, I stared up at the sky all night until I was interrupted.

"What are you doing way over here by yourself?" They asked as my eyes were watching God.

"I'm appreciating the beauty of God's creation. Have you seen the stars? The view is more beautiful in Finland than it is in America."

"Oh nice. Well you know, I have faith too." I looked at them. "Yeah, it's just hard right now though since the love of my life is going through medical issues and…" They choked up and broke down in tears. "I've been praying but it seems like they aren't getting answered." They apologized for the tears and thanked me for listening. My heart shifted and showed compassion.

"I don't know what you're feeling exactly, but I do know I serve a God that cares and loves you. Do you mind if I pray with you?" I asked as I grasped their hands. I lead them in a prayer that I believed changed their life forever.

Opportunity 4: Unfamiliar Territory

"God will not put you in the position of leadership until you take the position of servanthood."

-Schwartzen Precil

With my newfound appreciation for the wilderness, I took a job working at a bible camp in the summer of 2015. I drove up to the camp and it was like the Disney Movie "Camp Rock." I did not expect to be sleeping in the middle of the woods with ticks biting me. Working at a bible camp taught me the difference between religion and relationship.

At the bible camp is where I spoke to a group of white men and women for the first time about my dark past. Surprisingly, I was not judged, but they could not relate. I freely shared my testimony as often as possible. The more I spoke about my past, the better it felt being around them. It felt strange. The preconceived notion that people will not accept you because of your different upbringings proved to be false. Do not allow years of built up fear prevent you from sharing the message you have inside of yourself.

As I worked at the camp, I stopped playing basketball since I dedicated myself to teaching the word of God to the youth. People thought I lost my mind, but it was what I desired. It made me feel bad, but my coworker Sarah was very supportive. I supported her when she lost her grandfather back in her home country of Northern Ireland. She later returned the favor several years later by comforting me after a major fall out with my significant other.

Compassion

One of my campers was a 52-year-old cancer survivor named Joey Michael Jackson. He was one of the first people that asked me to pray for him. He opened about his struggles growing up. He depended on God to get through the pain. I took his hands and I led him in prayer and after I finished, he also prayed for me. Joey is a Hero in the Upper Peninsula community.

Things were well up until someone close to me called about the shooting where Dylan Roof killed black church members in South Carolina.

They said, "I fear for your life as you're up in the woods with those people."

Fear hijacked my mind as the thought of the camp staff potentially harming me came to mind. I walked around that morning both angry and bitter. I walked to the basketball court to clear my mind before the weekly staff meeting. I saw something that changed my life.

Written in chalk on the basketball court was my name. Next to my name was a letter.

"Schwartz, here is a gift. use your b-ball skills for God and for fun."

Out of all the emotions I felt, sympathy was the last one I expected to receive. My coworkers could not understand my pain, my frustration, my anger, or my situation. All I could think about was the words from the phone call. I was in for a surprise of a lifetime. The camp director started the meeting.

"There was a tragedy within the Evangelical Lutheran Church of America (ELCA)." She spoke.

My heart literally stopped.

"One of our sister churches was attacked by an individual who killed several black church members and leaders.

It was of racist intent and we need to pray for the lives and the families that were affected by this senseless killing."

Time stopped. I lost it. Within seconds of her words, I put my head down and gave the loudest cry I had in years. This was it. My moment of truth. The anger in my heart was replaced by the image of my name on the basketball court.

The words read "Schwartz," but my eyes saw love "LOVE." This was love, love at its finest. If I had never known God's love before that moment, I certainly did then. I wept loudly as the staff members watched in disbelief. It was the cries of built up silence. It was the cry of the voiceless and the oppressed. I developed the capacity to own and share my truth.

"This morning, I received a call from my people back in New York about the shooting in Charleston. I was angry at it because of what this country thinks of its Black citizens. I've always dealt with racism for as long as I can remember, and this is the first time it has ever been addressed. I thought I was coming to this meeting expressed my hate and anger but instead I see my name on the court and..." I choked up. "It's beautiful..." I cried some more, cried badly. I could not finish my sentences.

One by one, each of the staff gave me a hug, which I desperately needed. I felt each person's spirit. More importantly, I felt the spirit of God. The spirit of storge (a type of love in Greek). The Holy Spirit. Throughout the final weeks at the bible camp, I taught, coached, and trained campers from all different skill levels in basketball. The satisfied looks on the parents' faces gave me the answer I had been looking for. God wanted me to continue playing basketball.

Opportunity 5: Full attention

"Rock bottom may be the only obstacle where we get the opportunity to be fully attentive to what God has been showing us our entire lives."

-Schwartzen Precil

One of the common difficulties' life brings is the ability to see the glory in hitting rock bottom. When an individual experiences rock bottom it means they are at their lowest point in life. Situations cannot get any worse than rock bottom. Rock bottom can mean a jail cell, homelessness, bankruptcy, death of a loved one, being kicked out of school, hospitalized, a broken relationship etc. Those are very extreme cases, but rock bottom is an extreme scenario. I became all too familiar with extreme scenarios. When I nearly committed suicide as a freshman, God grabbed my attention.

I was removed from the culture of New York for a while and my sixth sense began to allow me to actively listen to how God led me. The noise was finally shut up and I cleared my mind. There is beauty knowing you cannot get any lower. Rock bottom is a grand opportunity for you to truly reset and reshape of life.

"True callings are heard from the heart not from the ear. Kill the noise of your flesh and your understanding becomes clear."

-Schwartzen Precil

With no experience in politics or policy making, the Dean of Students asked me to fill the student senate President position. Unsure of my capabilities I went to God to respond to the call of leadership. God positioned me to occupy the highest student government role as a young black male at a PWI where less than 10% of the student population was black or colored.

I appointed one of the most fearless guys I knew to be my VP, Zeke. Zeke became my right hand as he was extremely mature for his age. Zeke and I were basketball teammates but built a stronger bond when he became my vice president. I dedicated my summer learning how to unleash the leader within me. I could not afford to lose focus.

Driving dozens of times back and forth from Michigan to New York became a motivation to do anything. One time my 1997 Nissan Maxima flipped over the guardrail so fast I could hardly blink. The only thing I remembered was a bright white light flash right before the car landed in the snowbank. The following year my car slid into a ditch as I prayed to God for protection. My car was damaged, but I always managed to drive it across the country. God had protected me from death multiple times.

"Fall outs in relationships seem bad at the moment. It can be the exact turning point that you need to become the best version of yourself."

-Schwartzen Precil

David had called me about his own rock bottom obstacle with Lucy. He called me to tell me how Lucy kicked him out her dorm room at 2am in the middle of a snowstorm. He had to drive four hours through the snow to find a place to stay. I told him to leave her alone, but he said it was not anything out of the ordinary. He justified Lucy's actions and took her back weeks later only for Lucy to test his limits again.

Lucy's dance was dangerous. He clung to the idea of puppy love as a young adult. Lucy and David were travelled across the country one time when an argument broke out. Lucy put her finger on David's forehead provoking him to put his hands on her.

"What you gonna do hit me?! Come on, I dare you!" David was trapped by her words. He decided to pull over on the gas station to cool off. As soon as Lucy got out the car he drove off and called me. His emotions were through the roof as he told me the story. If a man puts their hands on a woman, it cannot be taken back. He had decided to let her go for a few years until they finally got back together.

Chapter 15: A Heroes' Fight

He who exalts himself will be humbled. He who humbles himself will be exalted.

Matthew 23:12 (NKJV)

As the Student Senate President, I studied the university handbook. I studied the Upper Peninsula history and geography. When I travelled to Finland, I met judges, teachers, business leaders, and the Mayor of Tampere, the second largest city in Finland. Mayor Ikonen greeted everyone with a handshake and a warm smile. She was a gracious woman who led with a spirit of humility. The elegance of her smile and the tone of her voice spoke volumes about her character.

The first words she said as she sat down were, "when I was a little girl..."

She seemed to be perfect by her genuine mannerism. I was impressed by her style of professional clothing that complemented her fashionable earrings. She gave enthusiastic feedback as my classmates and I shared our experiences in Tampere, Finland. I desired to model my leadership with the same humility she displayed. Her leadership showed sincerity, authenticity and true understanding. She mentioned how her moralistic values were her personal "superpowers."

A few days after the meeting, my classmates and I took a tour to a Finnish prison. There were no gates, guards or security check in. It looked to be more of a community center than a prison. My preconceived notion of prisons was barbed wire fencing with guards on standby to prepare for prison riots. So much for Hollywood movies. The people in prison cultivated their gifts by gardening, cooking, and studying for their degree. Finland does not treat its citizens poorly when they commit a crime.

***

I returned to the university with fire in my belly. I felt competent into being the leader God called me to be. Being the President of Student Senate, the President of the BSU club, a residential advisor, a college basketball player and a SISU seminar assistant can weigh heavy on the average person. I wanted to be above average.

The amount of black inner-city freshmen that arrived on campus for the football program was beyond my limits. My age, title, or status was meaningless to kids who grew up in the inner-city. To them, leading with humility was perceived as "soft." I opened up a conversation with the struggles of my upbringing. Being transparent about my life in the streets was the key to grasping their respect.

"Professional coaching is a necessity. Our blind spots need to be developed in order to maximize our influence."

-Schwartzen Precil

"You think surviving in the streets was hard? Wait until you learn how to survive up here. That street mentality doesn't fly up here fellas. College is where you find out what you're really made of. If you do not rid yourself of the inner-city mentality, you will not make it in college."

I spoke to the underclassman during the BSU opening meeting that year. My objective was to set the example for the underclassmen. It came with severe challenges as my actions needed to align with my words. I talked about my misfortunes more than my accomplishments. My upbringing was hard to believe based on how I represented myself.

I needed all the help I could get. I reached out to Michigan Tech's organizations to network with their Black Student Association (BSA) and African Student Union (ASU). I became a member of the National Society of Black Engineers (NSBE) chapter on Tech's campus to enhance my professionalism as a leader at a PWI. I felt like Fury calling on the Avengers for help as I searched the resources needed to lead effectively.

The hardest part about leading my peers was accepting that most of them were from low academically achieving school districts. Being that the underclassmen outnumber the upperclassmen 10 to 1, challenging is an understatement. I could not expect the underclassmen to be as disciplined. They were young, dumb, and wanted to have fun. Peer influence was a major liability. Many had a hard time balancing academics, sports, and extracurricular activities. The ones that were consistent I appointed them roles, responsibilities and collectively we hosted successful events on campus.

To whom much is given, much shall be required.

Luke 12:48

The first few months of the semester started strong, but I anticipated adversity to hit. I did not anticipate the scale in which the adversity happened. Many of the football players were involved in a brawl with the local community members. Some of the players were black some were white. Community members went to social media and threatened "to shoot the black football players." The great divide was finally exposed. If adversity was like a hurricane, this was a category five.

As a young black college student who had been discriminated against, their fight was my fight. I was one of two black leaders on campus in attendance. At the forum, they addressed issues, except the elephant in the room remained silent. The black football players and the white football players sat separately. I took the opportunity to address injustices and could harbor my truth no more. I spoke directly and intensely.

"This issue is bigger than a football brawl that took place last week. This affects everyone. I speak to my people affected by racism not as an RA, or the president of the BSU or student government but as a black man! A black man that grew up in poverty and I live in this rural white community as well. I've dealt with racism up here for years and it's time to say what needs to be said. There's too much division going on! We need unity from coaches, staff and community members if we plan to move forward from a racist societal system!"

There was no turning back. After I spoke, DRob spoke. If I was Dr. King addressing the situation, DRob was certainly Malcolm X. Things escalated quickly. Less than a week later, I walked through MTU's campus to attend a NSBE and received a text message.

"NSBE meeting canceled today. Stay off the campus sidewalks and streets. There was a threat to shoot all black people on campus. Be careful Schwartz, I hope you're not over here now."

Fear slithered down my spine. Paranoia kicked in as I stopped walking to look over my shoulder. Survival instincts kicked in as I saw a white student approaching. Fear reminded me that I had not escaped my past yet. The white male walked past me and did not notice my heart pounding through my chest. I walked to the Center of Diversity and Inclusion building where students and other community members gathered to discuss solutions to the threats. I arrived and a group of people sat in a circle where the NSBE advisor greeted me. I sat with the NSBE members and saw the diverse group of blacks, whites, Indians, natives etc. all gathered to support the black community.

They addressed the blackface party hosted by a white fraternity earlier in the semester. The threats on social media added fuel to the fire. The meeting ended with a plan of action to set up a community wide forum. A statement was made as the student who threatened to shoot black people on social media was acquitted of all domestic terrorist charges. White supremacy could no longer hide. As far as the justice system was concerned, our black lives didn't matter.

There was national recognition to the gentleman Jonathan Butler who had been on a hunger strike because of racial tensions at Missouri University. Jonathan was determined to force the university president, Tim Wolfe, to resign. Mr. Butler went weeks without food. His extreme actions resulted in the resignation of both the president and chancellor of the university. The event sparked a nationwide movement across college campuses where students of all backgrounds stood against injustice and inequality.

"The community waits for a person like you to educate us on topics we've always wanted to talk about."

-Anonymous

I attempted to push the university I attended in the movement. Both universities joined for the movement. Our NSBE organization executed a "Walk for Justice March." Hundreds stood hand in hand and chanted "We Stand as One!" as we marched through the town to the courthouse that acquitted the student who publicly threatened the lives of black citizens.

I continued my fight for justice and equality as I travelled to St. Louis, Missouri to attend a conference. The Christian fellowship group I went with were ignorant to what happened in their community. It was a true test of my faith since I witnessed white privilege among the people of God. Speakers like Patrick Fung, Francis Chan, David Platt, and Christena Cleveland primarily focused on the racial injustices around the country. It gave life to the reason why #BlackLivesMatter was part of my calling as a leader. A discussion panel about the Mike Brown shooting in Ferguson, MO was a main topic at the conference. Only a year prior, a white police officer gunned down an unarmed Mike Brown in the middle of the street. Witnesses who saw the shooting on August 9th, 2014 spoke at the panel.

"As if a voting ballot will change the events of what we all just saw. You cannot undo years of injustice and oppression by simply casting a vote. We need real unity!" One of the panel members spoke with conviction. I was one of disbelief as he mentioned how politicians used Mike Brown's death to push their agendas. Watching powerful activist Michelle Higgins, a St. Louis native, address core concerns about the killings of unarmed black men to a crowd of 15,000 people was an image that fueled my cause. She is a hero.

"Being a Christian means being an advocate for justice."

-Michelle Higgins

I pioneered the real change that needed to happen. I was relentless in the fight. Zeke and I made demands to the university upper administration. After weeks of back and forth emails, upper administration, Zeke and myself finally had a sit down. I looked them in the eyes and asked him with a sincere heart.

"Do you care about the black lives in this community?"

They answered without any hesitation, flinch, or pause, "yes, we do."

"Then let's make change happen. Meet the demands."

We walked out not knowing what to expect next. Less than a week later, the university announced an inaugural Martin Luther King Jr. Day of service on campus. It is a day where all class sessions are substituted for community service for the day. It honors and represents the values of the great Dr. King. The university organized community outreach to local businesses and hosted a panel discussion. All students, no matter where they came from, served the community in which they resided in.

The tradition did not exist at the university I attended prior to January 2016. We attempted to change policies but recognizing Dr. Martin Luther King Jr. was a step in the right direction. Our voices were heard. There will always be a need to celebrate the life of those who fought for human rights. It gives the entire world hope to keep fighting for a good cause. Dr. King gave his life for a dream he believed was worth dying for. Justice, equality, and basic civil rights.

"Injustice anywhere is a threat to justice everywhere."

-Dr Martin Luther King Jr.

It was the momentum needed to shift the community I was empowered to lead the change. When KD and Ms. Philly left the university, I was unsure of whether to continue the fight without them. Little did I know Ms. Fogle, my supervisor and mentor, had much fight in her. She took on the role as the BSU advisor.

Being a white lady from the Upper Peninsula, she took on the challenge of being a supporter of the movement. She affirmed me like a big sister and challenged me in ways that made me think. We finished the year strong with the 2nd Annual Diversity Dinner that the former BSU president enacted one year prior. Most of the inner-city underclassmen football players left the university. The BSU had little to no members as the following year I left to focus on a life-long goal to play European basketball while continuing my studies.

"At a certain point, you must abandon the rules imposed on you. Create new rules."

-Schwartzen Precil

When God opens doors for opportunity to serve others, expect there to be great obstacles. Obstacles can be discouraging, but with the right attitude and support is it possible to get through it. During my time as the president, I maximized my influence by speaking in ways I had never spoken before. I educated myself on the leaders within the bible and how there were bad leaders and good leaders. Proverbs 20:28 states "love and truth form a good leader; sound leadership is founded on loving integrity." I did my best to embody that style of leadership as I challenged myself to build my integrity.

1986, is the year MLK Jr. became a nationally recognized holiday. This was 15 years after his death. His fight for civil rights changed the pinnacle of human history but it took 15 years for America to declare such a beautiful day. When I attended college as a freshman in 2012, students went to class on MLK Jr. day. BSU members did not. We organized ourselves and displayed civil disobedience.

Four years later, my title as the Student Senate President put me in front of the decision makers. It took 30 years for the university I attended to implement Martin Luther King Jr. Day as a national holiday in 2016. It was a hard-fought journey and I had doubtful moments. I fought for two reasons outside of myself. Those who paved the way before us, and those who will come after us. That is a cause worth fighting for. That is true heroism.

Chapter 16: Heroic Spirit

Although the Lord gives you the bread of adversity and the water of affliction, your teachers will be hidden no more; with your own eyes you will see them.

Isaiah 30:20

As my responsibilities piled up over the years, I continued to use basketball to escape from my emotions. The college basketball program hired a new coach when I was a sophomore. I increased my training sessions as I set out to be a starter. The new head coach brought in his own recruits and treated me unfairly. I spent countless hours in the gym as I remained faithful with a morning routine of training every day before classes started.

Even my strong work ethic did not override the coaches' agenda to ensure his recruits more playing time. I went through a period of extreme bitterness as I spoke with the coach many times about the unfairness. To no avail. I took things into my own hands. I used my network to get me to Europe. One of my teammates was an exchange student who had experience playing European basketball.

He brought much positivity to the team by sharing his European basketball experience and suggested I go over to Finland if I wanted to play in Europe. I pursued the opportunity and went to play in Finland. The following year, I practiced with my first European basketball team and had a taste of high caliber basketball.

Straih brought me to his basketball practice and I was excited and nervous at the same time. The FIBA basketball felt different, the facility had many lines across the court. I was uncomfortable not knowing the language they spoke. After a few scrimmage games, Straih noticed that I was timid in my game play. Straih gave me a pep talk to get my head in the game. My team went on a winning streak and I showed a glimpse of my potential. It was the start of my basketball journey in Europe. I came back to play in Europe after my last year of college basketball.

During my final season as a college player, I trained the entire pre-season with 5 a.m. workouts, 3 days a week. I stayed true to the process and had outstanding performances that season. I put together a highlight film, a resume, and secured my spot in an annual showcase tournament with Straih. The tournament had coaches and players there from Finland's top basketball league in Finland.

At the awards banquet, Coach awarded me with the Most Improved Player award. After three all-academic teams, three varsity letters and the most improved player of the year award, my collegiate playing career was over. I increased the number of hours spent in the gym as I transitioned out of my leadership positions at the university.

"Mother Eagle pushes their eaglets out of the nest when it is time to fly. Some fall and die, others soar above the sky. God may be pushing you out the nest. You will not die so do your best."

-Schwartzen Precil

Returning to Staten Island in Summer 2016, I needed to train with someone who matched my passion and intensity for basketball. Someone to hold me accountable. Only one person came to mind, his name was Ant. He had a proven track record for hard work as his work ethic had led him to chase his dream of playing college basketball. It had been two years since we were in his backyard doing drills at 6am.

After we organized our schedules, we executed a 40-day execution plan of basketball drills, weightlifting, and muscle recovery to improve our game. We met at 4am every day to complete the "Kobe Workout." Trivet sponsored my efforts since I stayed consistent. The basketball drills consisted of cardio, weightlifting, and skill development between the hours of 4am and 11am. We rested mid-afternoon only to spend the evening shooting and playing pickup basketball. I monitored my time from sunup to sundown. We trained at the beach throughout the summer which nearly gave us a heat stroke.

We were amateurs at the professional level, but one coach took notice. The coach asked me about my goals with basketball and offered to help me improve. He introduced me to his son, who was a guru with experience training upper level athletes. His fierce gaze spoke volumes about his character and determination that showed through his training. This was bigger than basketball. His eyes read, *you sure you up for the challenge?* I shook his hand and the first words he said to me was "are you ready to work?"

I trained with the guru for the duration of time before I left the country. We trained with many of Staten Island's top high school, college and professional level basketball players. The more I trained with the guru, the more I soaked up his intelligence. Being around hungry basketball players made me hungrier. It was like a jungle as we fought tooth and nail to be the top dog.

I assisted Ant with his college basketball recruiting process. He came to me for advice as I helped him make career-changing decisions. Ant's first college workout at a Division I JUCO did not go as he anticipated. Players were selfish which did not match Ant's playing style. His emotions got the best of him and his anger became his worst enemy. It was too common among black men in the inner-city communities. He was upset at the coach for not using Ant's full capability. I believed in myself enough to take a leap of faith to go to Europe without the guarantee that I would play on a team.

"It is not their responsibility to place you in a position for success. It is your responsibility."

-Schwartzen Precil

Part of the process of being a great player is about accepting the unknown future of what teams may or may not be looking for. Traveling to Europe put me in a position to adjust create an opportunity of success for myself. Ant became irritated but played his freshman season till the end.

Hard work can sometimes create a false expectation that you will receive the results you desire. There are millions of people that show extreme effort for opportunities that lead to disappointments. Effort is a consistent action that does not guarantee results.

Two weeks before my departure, a 7th grade basketball player and I showed up to workout with the Guru. With only two people at training, the Guru did not give us much rest time in between drills. It was the most intense training of the summer. Either Guru was upset that day, or the other trainee and I were off our game. We repeated drills dozens of times. After about the 30th time of doing the same drill my body began to give way. My legs felt like noodles and my arms could no longer take the pain. I heard the inner voice talk to me and ask me as clear as day, *is it worth it Schwartz?*

The Guru pushed me to the point where I heard the voice of truth. *Basketball was only a game. I have more to offer than my physical abilities.* My lungs felt like they were about to collapse. I was seconds away from dropping the basketball and walking out of the gym. The Guru increased the intensity. I was mentally and physically exhausted and tuned him out. A ringing noise kicked in as my vision blurred.

I slouched over with my hands on my knees gasping for air. I could feel my body no more. The thought to quit crossed my mind for a second time as the Guru continued to use his words to motivate physical limitations. With my hands on my knees, I looked over my right shoulder and saw that the 7th grade trainee crying as their mother watched them in pain. She looked as exhausted as I was. I stared silently as I watched her mother gaze at her daughter's determined spirit. The gaze spoke as if the mom on the bench spoke the words, "don't give up."

I looked at the guru who waited for me to pick up the basketball and finish the drill.

"Water," I gasped.

"No water until you both complete this drill!" Guru boomed as the 7th grader picked up the ball and began the drill. I followed up. We managed to finish the drill and the 7th grader's mother bought us both Gatorades. Guru went up to the 7th grader and said, "That's why UConn is going to recruit you. Moments like these are going to set you apart from the rest of the girls."

He turned his head to look at me. "That's why you're going to be a professional basketball player; moments like this are going to show why you're different from those other ball players Schwartz. You are built like a bull and you're raw. No one trained you growing up and so you have to show coaches your value comes from your gift of work ethic. That's your gift, a relentless work ethic."

***

I arrived in Finland and was greeted by Straih at the airport. Straih and I trained for a couple of days up until the tournament started. When we arrived at the stadium, I took a deep breath during the layup line. Someone said, "yo, we're playing (I forget his name) the Finnish national championship point guard in the first game!" My competitive instincts kicked in. I came off the bench prepared to match up with the 2016 Finnish champion point guard. I checked into the game the point guard looked right at me. It was a physical game where I finished my first European basketball game with 16 points. We lost every game in the tournament, but it did not discourage me from talking to coaches and organizations. I networked my way around to different basketball clubs until I found one in Jyvaskyla, Finland. It was the hometown of current Chicago Bulls player, Lauri Markannen.

***

I attended several team workouts in Jyvaskyla, Finland with multiple basketball clubs. I trained with an American coach who formerly coach of a rebranded team called Jyvaskyla Basketball Academy (JBA). Their new coach Mikko imparted wisdom and insight during my time in Finland. Coach Mikko and I shared many conversations about our faith. With his help, I decided to commit to play with Jyvaskyla Weikot (JyWe) club for the 2016-2017 season.

Outside of basketball, I attended classes at a Finnish University called JAMK. I was the only American out of the hundreds of students that studied business. There were students from Germany, Italy, France, the Netherlands, England, Turkey, etc. During one of my Cross-Cultural Management courses, refugees told incredibly heroic stories.

During my training session my Russian teammate asked me a pivotal question. "What's your dream?"

"What?" I asked.

"What's your dream? Like what's the one thing you dreamed of doing when you were younger?" He reiterated.

I told him the first thing that came to mind. "Well, I'm living my dream. I play basketball in a foreign country. Of course, I want to play in the NBA, but look where I am. I'm from Staten Island, where ball players dream about playing European basketball. I'm living my dream. What's your dream?"

"I want to have a good life, you know. Sports are good, yes, and dance I love, but I want a happy family. I am a Finnish championship dancer. I left my country at 15-years-old to dance and moved in with my girlfriend. We broke up and so I stopped dancing. Dance and basketball is great, yes but to have a family, that is the dream."

His answer made me think. *What was my dream? Did I really want to play basketball as bad as I did when I was younger?* I was under the illusion that I had been living my dream. The dream I created was superficial. It was the narrative of the American Black Boy Dream of dribbling a ball to get away from the negativity in the neighborhood. Playing basketball was not my dream. Other than finding my family, I did not have one.

"It was all a dream..."

-Biggie Smalls

I averaged 25.5 points per game which was good for the second leading scorer in the entire Central Finnish League. I lead the team to a 5-2 record in the first seven games of the season. I scored a career high 38 points in one game and ended my last game of the season with my first career triple double. I was offered by a team to move to a higher division. The warden passed away while I was in Finland, I lost my reason to play basketball. The game no longer mattered to me.

I decided to visit Zay Wilks who played for BC Nokia in Finland. Spending time with him and his teammates cleared my head as it gave me a fresh perspective on my situation. As a veteran professional player from Staten Island, Zay was nothing short of a hero to us younger players. His help allowed me to finish the season on a strong note. I also spent time with Straih in Porvoo, Finland. After his game, I spoke with his American teammates about how they deal with personal problems being far away from home. The information I gathered allowed me to form my own opinion.

"Callings often dwell within well before you are conscious about them."

-Schwartzen Precil

Zeke had called me dozens of times while I was out of the country. Every call was a negative report about how bad things were at the university. Several black students were kicked out of school from an altercation. Some were BSU members, and the student who occupied the BSU president position struggled as a leader. My calling was back in America, not playing international basketball. My presence was needed elsewhere. I felt a bit responsible for the chaos as some of the guys who were kicked out were my good friends. I knew I had to return to my calling as a leader on campus.

Chapter 17: Heroes Need Help

In America, I had multiple encounters with the police. Most of them were on traffic stops. Being from New York, I was often profiled as "suspicious" looking. One time I was pulled over with my friends in the car and the police officer asked me a series of questions that clearly indicated profiling. We were four black young males riding in a black car at 11pm.

"Do you have any outstanding tickets? Are there any warrants out for your arrest? Do you have any previous major incidents on your driving record? Do you have any points on your license?"

I answered "no" to the questions. The voice of my foster mother peeked through my mind. *Stay away from the police.*

I went to grab my insurance card from the glove box. I had a black bag in the glovebox. "What's in that bag?" "The officer asked. My heart jumped.

I was careful not to reach in the bag. My boys in the car tensed up. I flipped the black bag upside down where the condoms fell out onto my lap. He then asked a question that solidified my assumption of being profiled.

"Any baby mama drama going on there pal? Why are you driving around with a bag full of condoms?" His prejudice question triggered some unexpressed emotions.

Another encounter was at the neighborhood gas station with a friend in my car at 9pm. Several unmarked cars pulled in front and behind my car. *Robbery!* I thought as I hit the pedal to speed off. I was half a second from speeding off when I heard police sirens. The unmarked vehicles were undercover police officers. I pulled over. Officers ran to the car with their guns halfway out of their holsters.

My friend and I were told to get out of the car. We were searched. To say I was scared would be an understatement. We all heard about traffic stops going wrong in the news.

One time I drove to the university during my final semester. I was reintroduced to what it meant to be a black man in America. The drive was smooth until a police car tailed me for a mile before pulling me over. I rolled down all my windows.

"You know why I'm stopping you?" The officer asked.

"No."

"You're driving a vehicle with no insurance. I ran your plate information and it says you have no insurance."

"What? Can I show you my insurance information? It's in the glove box." He nodded in agreement. I handed him the insurance information.

He looked at it. "Where ya coming from and where ya headed to?"

"I was actually out of the country in Europe for the past seven months. I'm from New York but I'm headed to my school in the Upper Peninsula." I answered.

After carefully examining my license and insurance information, he told me to sit tight as he walked to his vehicle. He walked away and was back within 10 minutes.

"Do you mind stepping out of the vehicle?"

"Wait why?" I asked in a concerned tone. Not the wisest question to ask an officer.

"Get out of the car now!" His voice exploded and as I was at his mercy. I stepped out of the car.

"Hands on the hood!" He patted me down, grabbed my wrists and placed me handcuffs. "You're under arrest for operating a motor vehicle on a state highway without insurance."

I did not have time to think before he asked me the next question. "What are you hiding back there?" He referred to my boxes in the back of my car.

"What? That's my stuff I'm taking back to college." My voice screeched as another squad car pulled up behind the officer's vehicle.

"Your motor vehicle officially belongs to the County sheriff's department is there any contraband in the car? Any methamphetamine, opioids, heroin, cocaine," and he named about six other drugs that I had never heard of. I answered 'no.'

He then proceeds to get in my face and say, "What do you have in the car? Whatever you're hiding I'm going to find it! I will tear that car apart piece by piece if I have to."

He was frustrated and attempted to force a false confession from me. I stood my ground by denying any drugs being in the car. As he walked into my vehicle, the other officer grabbed me and placed me in the back of the squad car. I watched as he rummaged through my belongings.

What if he plants something in the car? What if he doesn't let me go after he doesn't find anything? What if he gets angrier because he doesn't find anything? The negative thoughts flooded my mind as I watched the officer tear apart pillowcases, empty out boxes, and completely disrespect my property. *Was he legally able to do that?* My arms were cuffed behind my back as I watched my belongings get thrown around with no sense of value.

Back in New York, it is so common for a police officer to "find" something once they searched the vehicle. The officer came back to his vehicle and drove me to the county jail. It felt unreal until a mugshot and fingerprints were taken.

The guard in the booking cell spoke. "Aye man, you're really not supposed to go to jail for a non-insured vehicle but since so many other people who look like you drive through our county with drugs the officer assumed you were a trafficker. That guy can be a real a**hole sometimes, so don't take it too personal. 80% of the guys at this jail are serving for drug related charges, you dodged a bullet."

I was profiled as a drug dealer. Talk about misfortune. *Where are you God?* The day I was arrested, I was supposed to make an appearance at the university for the second annual Martin Luther King Jr day of service. Instead, I spent the next 16 hours lying on a cot with four other inmates.

I spoke to the other inmates in the holding cell. One guy had served two years and was about to be released in a few hours.

"Did you find God within the two years you served here?" I asked him.

"Man, I read the Bible, the Torah, the Kuran, and the book of Morman and none of them did sh*t for me. I was locked up for a drug raid in South West, Detroit. God doesn't exist."

I responded by sharing the story of how God showed up in my dorm room as a college freshman.

"Let that sh*t go dawg." His Detroit accent came out. "God ain't listening to people who are all messed up like me. Look at you. You here cause you black. If my white a** was out there driving with no insurance, you think they would've arrested me? I got caught from a police raid, not from a damn traffic stop. Ain't no way He's real."

Fear spoke, *he could be right.* The thought was entertained by being served nasty food in the cell, sleeping on a nasty cot, and being in the room with four other men not knowing what could happen. My faith was in jeopardy. Trivet took a seven-hour drive from Buffalo, NY to bail me out.

The miracle chronicles

I called KD as he drove from a church van with no valid license plate from Detroit two hours to where I was. The van battery died several times, and we were stuck on the side of the road in 20-degree weather. We prayed for a miracle and received several. A man pulled over to help us jumpstart the battery. I purchased a new battery praying that it would hold off to make it past the Mackinac Bridge where. We drove 45 minutes with no headlights in the middle of the dark as the car battery slowly died. We arrived at the Mackinac Bridge and the van shut off. KD, his nephew and I were stuck on a 5-mile long bridge with no hazard lights, at 25-feet above the water in the middle of the dark; a recipe for disaster. By the grace of God, a gentleman in a pickup truck pulled over and towed us across the bridge into the McDonalds' parking lot where we waited for Zeke to pick us up.

With no time to reflect or process the traumatic events, I searched right away for a job. I had to save money to go to court where I faced a hefty fine. I took a job with the maintenance team waking up at 5am to shovel snow. On top of the job, I had 9am class, and a 25-hour per week internship. With no car, little money, and a graduation deadline, I prayed day in and day out.

One day during my internship, I recognized a woman from the Bible camp I worked at.

"How are things going Schwartz?" She asked.

I looked into her eyes and felt compelled to tell her the truth.

"Not good. A few weeks ago, I was arrested for driving with no insurance. I have court next week and I have to pay the fine, but the courts repossessed my car and I have no way to get there. I've been praying to God, but He hasn't made a way yet. I asked the courts to extend my time but there was nothing they could do. Soon I'll have a warrant out for my arrest."

"Wow Schwartzen. Maybe I can help; I'll take your number down and give you a call after I talk to my husband." I did not think anything of it until the following day. I received a call from her.

"My husband and I can let you borrow our car to drive downstate next week and if you need to stay at our home, you're more than welcome to."

I cried from that miracle as God answered my prayers. I paid a total of $900 for the case to be dismissed. After finally paying off the fine for the tickets, I opened up to my landlord on why I was unable to pay rent for the past two months. I sat down with him to tell him the truth about me getting pulled over, my car being repossessed, and why I was unable to pay rent. He was an older guy with a big heart who was unafraid to speak his mind, truth, or wisdom. His story of how he nearly died after a motorcycle accident gave me motivation that anything is possible.

His entire body was once completely dismantled, yet he managed to help others in their time of need. He offered a book for me to read called "The Prophet." That book led me to call my high school coach to help me pay overdue rent. I asked a nontraditional full-time student, who was also a member to help me rebuild the BSU. Her story of how she beat cancer was incredible as she was married with several children yet agreed to help provide her services of cooking. Reaching out for help was a crucial point to rebuilding the BSU.

"Pride is the first chapter in the book of failure. Humility is the first chapter in the book of success."

-Mark Batterson

I took an African American literature course during my final semester. The professor was not black, and it was the first year the university had offered a course on African American literature. Her course opened my eyes to black authors like Ta-

Nehisi Coates, Zora Neal Hurston, and Toni Morrison. I fell in love with reading and literature all over again.

On personal time, I read Martin Luther King Jr.'s book titled "Why We Can't Wait." It was the necessary book I needed to read to allow me to move past my trauma of going to jail. Dr. King wrote about a time where he was doubtful during his time as a civil rights leader. Hence, the letter to his fellow Clergymen called his civil disobedience "untimely."

After I read his frustrating words in the book, I was able to see the human side of him. His fight for human rights put a strain on the relationship between him and his wife. His rock bottom obstacle was the time spent in the Birmingham, AL jail cell. He thought about possibly calling the civil disobedient protest off as he sat in jail. Dr. Martin Luther King, Jr. had low moments that were not publicized for good reason. When I read, he was not perfect, but someone flawed led by God in his calling as a minister.

My grace is sufficient for you, for my power is made perfect in weakness.

2 Corinthians 12:9

Dr. King's expression during his weak moments is what gave me hope to be a great leader. Belief is a powerful tool that people can use to get through the challenges. Dr. King is one of the greatest heroes of all time. His expression of grief to his fellow clergymen about their betrayal became part of my healing process. I needed to let my truth out somehow someday, why not a book like Dr. King. I had a voice and it needed to be heard before I left my university.

"I either find a way or make a way."

-Hannibal Lecter

After receiving the Sampo Society award, SiSU award, the outstanding senior award, I applied for the student representation award. My advisor fought tooth and nail, and my credentials spoke volumes, but I came up short for the overall GPA requirements. I had a 3.79 cumulative GPA and I needed a 3.9. Shout out to my freshman year academics.

I was unable to give a speech at graduation, so I asked God to make a way for me to speak. I believed God had prepared a speech in my heart to give. If you have made it this far in the book, you should know by now, I do not take "no" for an answer.

The morning of graduation Trivet drove 20 hours through the night with my adopted family members. I received a phone call saying they may miss me walking across the stage because of the long drive. I was reminded of my life's disappointment on the biggest day of my life. I sat with Ms. Fogle office moments before the ceremony.

"My family drove all the way from New York and won't be able to see me walk across the stage." I told her as I fought back tears.

"I'm sorry, Schwartz. Hopefully, they will make it, you've come a long way in five years, don't allow this moment to go to waste. Do me a favor. When you're in your cap and gown, just take a moment. Take a moment to be present. You've accomplished a long-term goal. Five years of college to be at a graduation that lasts two hours. Make those hours count. I'll be in the stands watching my two boys (Zeke and I) get their degrees. Love you Schwartz, I'm proud of you."

"I love you too Mama Fogle." I gave her a hug as my adopted family arrived at the campus. Straih flew out from Finland to America to see me walk across the stage. My emotions were all over the place. Thankfully, Miss Fogle's thoughtful words penetrated my mind as I sat in the chair listening to each speaker during the ceremony. During one of the speeches, I closed my eyes, prayed to God and felt sensational when I opened them. The image of me giving a speech on graduation popped into my head. At that moment, I felt more than a scholar or a college graduate.

They called my row to head to the stage and I began to think about Mr. Jarmond and how I wished he were there to watch me prove him wrong. Tears filled my eyes as they said my name "Schwartzen Lormand Jarmond." I walked up the stage and could no longer hold the emotions I had built up.

I walked on stage, turned to the right and walked over to the microphone. Words flowed from my mouth that I was unable to control. I Stood over a sea of people only to piece together sentences that I could not comprehend. The only words I recall saying was calling my professors "superheroes." I gave Mama Fogle her due acknowledgement as the crowd of thousands stood silent during my impromptu speech. I could not receive my diploma in peace without saying my final farewell believing I would be forgotten after graduation.

After the ceremony, I was greeted by professors and community members who thanked me for my kind words. When I looked in Trivet's eyes, I knew he was proud of me for not only graduating but also for bouncing back from my world of pain. Only he knew my true story. Only he knew the realness of how tough life was for me growing up. Now, I share my story with the world.

My first official speaking engagement was at the MiCapp leadership conference called "Anything is Possible." The following year at the same conference, I gave my presentation called "Leave your Legacy." I challenged the audience to believe in themselves, yet I still failed to believe in my full capabilities since I was 22-years-old and did not know what was next.

What is SISU?

European history shows Finland as this small group of people on a massive amount of land stuck between Sweden and Russia. Finland was once a neglected country that fought their way out of the control from other European empires. As a freshman in college, I took a class called SISU Seminar. I was afraid to talk about my upbringing but the SISU seminar class gave me time to write and reflect on my experience.

I hope all this talk about the SISU seminar had evoked the question of "What is SISU?" I'm glad you asked. I'll use it in a sentence. The Finns used "SISU" to overcome the 25 to 1 odds against Russia during the Winter War in 1939. If bravery, courage, perseverance, and persistence had a baby, it would be called "SISU." That's a fine line from crazy as the small country of Finland faced a super-powered country. SISU is a word of its own that captures the true spirit of the fighting underdog. It's the same way Buster Douglass knocked out the undefeated heavyweight champion Mike Tyson in 1990. The odds are never in favor of the underdog.

Chapter 18: The Hero's Rabbit Hole

And we know that all things work together for the good of those who love God, who are called according to His purpose.

Romans 8:28

The day after graduation, I went to my room after celebrating. I sat down to think, and one question came to mind, *now what?* I took a position with TRiO Upward Bound as an RA and became a mentor to high school students. I postponed living in the real world with a "9 to 5" job up until I found an organization that stood for what I believed, AmeriCorps; a federal funded program that fights to eradicate poverty. I found a great community in Grand Rapids, MI where I became a Volunteer in Service to America (VISTA) for AmeriCorps.

The summer after I graduated, I isolated myself by training for 40 days to prepare for professional basketball opportunities. I performed at a showcase tournament and was selected First Team all-tournament. I travelled to several professional basketball team showcases for the D-League and North American Basketball League (NABL) I signed a one-year contract and joined the Grand Rapids basketball team. I redeemed myself, as basketball was a true goal for me.

I balanced my playing opportunities with my calling as I lived in Grand Rapids, MI. There was no doubt in my mind that God wanted me to work with at risk youth. The nonprofit organization I joined was a diversion program. My first high school student was a young black male. He enrolled in my character-coaching course I taught as a young teenager on probation. He was nearly kicked out of school for stealing a phone from another student. When he violated the terms of his probation, he was sent off to a juvenile detention center.

I went to visit him, but he could not look me in the eyes. The visit was short, but his words were powerful.

"Mr. S, you were right. I should have listened to you." He walked away and I never saw him again.

I believed I was walking in my calling as well as pursuing basketball. I accomplished every goal I set out to achieve. *Why did I feel unfulfilled?* I went through a phase called the "post-graduation blues." The lack of fulfillment cultivated negative thoughts. My high school sweetheart and I were broken up for two years, then out of nowhere she asked to move in with me. Thinking it was the answer to my prayer, I moved her and all her possessions across the country. It opened an obstacle for a slow downward slope towards rock bottom.

I attempted to pick up where we left off in high school blinded the true vision God had for me. Attempting to rekindle a relationship with someone you are not supposed to be with is like giving mouth to mouth CPR to a corpse. God showed me all the red flags within that relationship that I decided to ignore. It took less than nine months for me to be homeless after creating a great life for myself.

In January 2018, I had a new car, a place to stay, great income, a professional basketball contract and I regularly attended church. When I moved my high school sweetheart in I became financially stressed. By Sept 2018, I was two months behind on rent, without a car, job, and no longer had my basketball contract. My failed attempt at marrying my high school sweetheart girl cost me relationships with close friends, family, and my livelihood suffered badly. A divorce followed shortly after. She had her parents to go back home to and Trivet picked up the pieces of my bad decision to move her in.

During my time of distress, I thought traveling out of the country could ease the pain, but it only made things worse. The contracts offered in Spain did not pay enough to support the both of us. I gave my best effort to make something out of an ugly situation. I managed to contact my good friend Sarah who supported me over the years. She allowed me and my girl to stay with her and her family. After my girl disrespected Sarah's household, she had severe mental illness. I was stuck between a rock and a hard place as my girl left me. Sarah comforted me in my time of need.

"Schwartzen, when I met you, you had this twinkle in your eye." Sarah said. "You helped me so much when I grieved for the passing of my Papa John. I want to see you thriving again like you were at the bible camp we worked at"

"The twinkle is not there anymore is it?" I asked shamefully.

"The twinkle is there. It's just hidden beneath your pain."

Her encouraging words reminded me of my worth. I was 24 years old, homeless, and still had a lot to offer. Her words were the spark I needed. The reminder of the twinkle was the moment I began to dream again. I did not know what the dream was, but I knew there was one. I could not see my dream at one point, but Sarah could. I travelled back to America and Trivet allowed me to stay on his couch after a disagreement between my adopted family and I led to a major fallout.

***

At 24-years-old, I left with a suitcase, my passport and a shattered heart. I worked in retail and spent six months on Trivet's couch. I felt like the scum of the earth, yet I continued to pray. I had no issue finding a semi-pro team to play for, but I was still unfulfilled, so I wrote this book. I made it my priority to find out where I came from since I had no family to talk to. I needed to know who I was as I looked in the mirror every day and did not recognize my reflection. Being young and black, I felt ashamed as I worked at a bookstore as I wrote and played semi-pro basketball.

My accountability partner called me one day.

"Aye dawg, you a grown a** man. Don't no one feel sorry for you. Who the hell is gonna read a book from a broke homeless dude who sleeps on his brother's couch?"

His tough love was my turning point. He lacked empathy, but he was truthful. I no longer licked my wounds as I saw my opportunity in my rock bottom obstacle one last time. Prior to empowering the youth at the Boys and Girls club, I took a job at the gym as I ignited my people skills again. Being a hopeless romantic my only hope to live depended on finding my biological family. I went on the search for them with everything I had.

I envisioned myself seeing my mother and father one day if I found them. In the Marvel movie Black Panther, there is a scene where N'Jadaka (Played by Michael B. Jordan) comes to the country of Wakanda in his alias as Eric Killmonger. He came to Wakanda with a heart full of revenge as his family abandoned him. As a boy, N'Jadaka's father was killed by his own brother. From that point, N'Jadaka sought to kill the Black Panther and become the king of Wakanda. His revenge proved to be the turning point of the movie as he announced himself to the blood cousin of the Black Panther speaking in his native tongue of Wakanda.

That scene imprinted the image in my mind on how I imagined myself meeting my long-lost family. I picture myself demanding my birth rights. I held on to that image for too long as it took N'Jadaka nearly two decades to finally take his revenge. That's nearly 20 years of plotting, thinking, and allowing revenge sit on his heart. 20 years of unexpressed trauma. Revenge always rots the heart. My own heart began to rot. I punched Trivet one time from the unexpressed revenge I had built up. Life was unfair.

After six months in isolation, I got back to my feet and began to walk in my calling to empower at risk youth. Trivet and I moved into a two bedroom together. My semi-pro coach provided a bed for my new place, and I saw the light at the end of the tunnel. After numerous calls to courts, filed paperwork, visiting social services to find my birth mom, it led to a dead end.

On April 30th, 2019, I finished writing the last page of this book and made a final call to a former foster parent where I demanded to know my mother's first name. That piece of information cracked the code I had been dying to figure out. I took my information to Dr. Google and the rest was history. I heard my mother's voice for the first time, and I got the healing I demanded out of life.

After all the years of not knowing the blood family, it turns out I did have more family than I can count. My relentless spirit led to a rabbit hole that made Trivet jump into action as he too found family. He and I were the lost brothers our family had been looking for. The adoption during adolescence changed our social security number and our birth given names. No one was able to find us for 25 years.

All the drama from the past was behind us as our big brother, Kalimah Priforce, was our mother's only son who was alive and well. My biological father's name was Privat Precil who died in March 2013. I heard he was a true renaissance man who had more than 14 children in his lifetime. Privat Precil was a writer, a lawyer, and nearly a pastor since he took seminary classes. My father was an avid dancer as well which is where I got my young dance moves from. My mother was a phenomenal athlete at both soccer and basketball which is where I got my love for athletics from.

I now know where I come from. I know what blood runs through my veins. I know that I am cared for. One thing I learned throughout the process of finding my relatives was that no one was going to do the dirty work for me. Most people were content but I, Schwartzen Young Precil, my mother's youngest son could not rest when the dust settled.

We each have the opportunity to be our own heroes in the journey through life. The foster care system was common for many people in my family including my uncle Joslin. With the help of God, he found his way to his long-lost family 25 years prior to being reunited with my long-lost family. I come from a family of true heroes as we all had overcome much pain. I come from a lineage of real-life heroes.

This book is a declaration of separation to the narrative I was told as a young black boy. I divorce the lies, manipulation, and deceit I was fed. To all those who are looking for their truth and continue to face opposition, look to God and He will lead the way. The answer in which you seek is closer than you think. He will make a way for you to realize your own truth.

I am 24 years old, writing an inspirational self-help book as if I'm 55-years-old. I share it with those who understand that there is a bigger purpose to your pain. It starts with being honest with yourself. The truth hurts a lot, but it does not hurt more than years of built up lies.

If you're waiting for a hero to do it for you, it might not come. I used to think my birth mom would kick down the door one day and take me out of the system. I used to wait for Trivet and I to team up and take down the evil warden and the other foster kids. Neither of those things happened. It took years of significant emotional experiences that brought me to the secret of my breakthrough. It was not about me when I found my family; it was about breaking the curse that led to healing and restoration for the generations to come. There comes a time when we must take full responsibility. Inaction is a choice; you may not be conscious of it, but it is still a choice. Make the choice to take responsibility. Be Your Own Hero and turn your obstacles into opportunities.

Author Bio:

As a 2019 American Book Fest award finalist for YA Non-fiction, "Be Your Own Hero: Turning Obstacles into Opportunities," has taken the literary world by storm. The author discovered the power of transforming adversity into positive energy after being placed in foster care by his first birthday. Schwartzen Precil, erupted as a mentor and community leader as an AmeriCorp VISTA after his undergraduate studies. Specializing in leadership curriculum development, his advocacy for erasing poverty has produced healthier outcomes for low opportunity youth and their families.

Website: www.heroleadershipgroup.com

Instagram: Schwartzen_828

Twitter: Schwartzen_828

Facebook: Schwartzen Precil

Acknowledgments

All glory be to Jesus Christ my Lord and savior. Thank you for the guidance and wisdom from your word as I trust you with my life. All glory belongs to you. To the ones that are looking down from heaven. Idrissa, Papa John, and my big brother Charlemagne aka Kino.

Trivet, the only blood I ever knew growing up. You more than made up for our fractured childhood relationship. You are my greatest role model and I love you. Let's welcome the rest of our lives with the newfound family we have. In the words of the late Nipsey Hussle "the marathon continues."

Thank you to the mother figures in my life:

Cynthia, for caring for Trivet and I for many years. You will always be "mommy" to me. I am forever grateful for you. Mama Grace, your wonderful words and outstanding support over the years. Best believe you are my hero. Mama Fogle, you believed in my potential and I thank you for your strength and wisdom over the years. Mama Dar, thank you for your wisdom over the years as we continue to fight for our faith daily.

Thank you to my sister figures:

Big sis Fatima for listening to her "crazy" intuitions, they're a gift from God as you made the pit more bearable. You are a true wounded warrior that stayed strong through it all. Reiana, thank you for believing in me all these years, your loyalty is not forgotten. Cousin Gladys who I can go to for anything.

Thank you to my coaches:

Coach Eliott for stepping up to be the father figure role in high school years. Coach Palma for your ability to see my strengths on and off the court. Coach Gerry Mosley for strengthening my skills and sending daily readings to help grow my faith. Coach Mikko for the opportunity to play and practice at a high level within Finland. Coach Matt (Guru) Reeves for the wisdom you imparted into me over the years. You are truly a light to those who can't quite see the potential we have within ourselves. Your consistency is unmatched as you have made "Kingship" the standard for many others like me.

To my brothers from other mothers:

Emeka for being a consistent positive influence on me. Demitri for being that peer role model on and off the basketball court. Brendon, for always being that brother figure throughout high school and beyond. Austin (AWill) Wilson you're the real hero as you continue to be a role model husband, father, and a brother to me and the rest of your family.

Anthony for staying consistent over the years and helping me unleash my true potential on and off the basketball court. DeeBrown for being my first peer role model and brother to me beyond college. Big Zeke, thank you for being a true friend when I needed it most. Kevin (KD), our spiritual discipline did not go in vain. We are faithful until the end as we are true warriors in the Lord. Terrance, thank you for being a continuous inspiration to me. Kevin Straih for the brotherhood we built that goes beyond basketball.

Thank you to my professors:

"College is a marathon, not a sprint. Learn self-discipline as it triumphs self-interest."

-Doctor Richard Gee.

Dr. Gee who helped open my mind to the truth. Dr. Porteen for being the hero that you are with your victory with breast cancer. Dr. Virtanen you showed me the true meaning of SISU by challenging me beyond my limits. Dr. MaryJane for being the best advisor anybody can ask for.

To my communities of International Christian Center, Finlandia University, Michigan Tech University, NSBE community, BSU community, Hancock, MI. Grand Rapids, MI. Staten Island, Bronx, Brooklyn, NY community. Finland community.

Special thanks:

Bobby Friedman for your willingness to talk about John Lennon as his hero and supporting me throughout my basketball career. Aaron Green for your spiritual wisdom Rik Koski aka "the man of steel" as you survived death multiple times. One of the most forgiven men I have met. Sarah Robinson and her family who have the biggest hearts anyone can ask for. The Rasners and the Holmgens for your large hearts.

Brandon (BeeRoni) for being a brother to me throughout college as I discovered "Eudaimonia" because of you. I thank BRob for staying true to yourself as one of a kind teammate. Cindy Cowell for being the mentor I needed in college, Kailee Laplander for the strength you show day in and day out. Michael Daniels for your ability to see great leadership within me. Erica for supporting me in my journey to find my family.

To my new found family: Matushca, Riva, Vivien, Viaud, Joslin, Jelani, Damian, Marvin, Consuelo, Gabby, Elijah, Noelle, Surge, the Cantave's, Precil's, and Gourgue's family as well as the rest of my newfound village from Haiti, Haitian-American and Afro-Latino community.

Reference Page

The copyright date of Action Comics #1 was registered as April 18, 1938. New Series, Volume 33, Part 2: Periodicals January-December 1938. United States Library of Congress. 1938. p. 129. <https://en.wikipedia.org/wiki/Superman>

Hugh Armitage. June 1 2019. Here's how to watch the entire X-Men movie series in chronological order. Retrieved Oct 2018 <https://www.digitalspy.com/movies/a844881/x-men-chronological-order-timeline/>

Imdb, 2004. Retrieved October 1 2018 <https://www.imdb.com/title/tt0316654/plotsummary>

Eric Thomas. Retrieved October 1 2018. <https://quotefancy.com/quote/1579046/Eric-Thomas-Don-t-quit-You-re-already-in-pain-You-re-already-hurt-Get-a-reward-from-it>

Imdb 2018. Retrieved Nov 3 2018. <https://www.imdb.com/title/tt1825683/plotsummary>

Quotes by Malcolm X. Retrieved Nov 11 2018. <https://www.malcolmx.com/quotes/>

Melanie Curtin. Writer, activist. May 10 2017. Retrieved Nov 13 2018
<https://www.inc.com/melanie-curtin/bill-gates-says-this-is-the-safest-age-to-give-a-child-a-smartphone.html>

Imdb 2018. Retrieved Nov 2018.
<https://www.imdb.com/title/tt1345836/plotsummary>

Genuis.com. Retrieved Nov 2018
<https://genius.com/Kendrick-lamar-poetic-justice-lyrics>

Brainy Quotes. Retrieved Dec 2018
https://www.brainyquote.com/authors/desmond-tutu-quotes

Cutler Michael, Preven Anee. AZLyrics. Retrieved Dec 2018
https://www.azlyrics.com/lyrics/beyonceknowles/listen.html

All Poetry. Retrieved Dec 2018
<https://allpoetry.com/The-Rose-That-Grew-From-Concrete>

Urban Dictionary April 2014. Retrieved Dec 2018
<https://www.urbandictionary.com/define.php?term=Situationship>

The Editors of Encyclopaedia Britannica. Virginia Gorlinski, Associate Editor. Retrieved Jan 2019.
<https://www.britannica.com/topic/Eros-Greek-god>

Genius. Retrieved Jan 2019
<https://genius.com/Eminem-love-the-way-you-lie-lyrics>

A.R. SHAW. March 2017. Retrieved Jan 2019
<https://rollingout.com/2017/03/09/8-powerful-lyrics-biggie-smalls-will-motivate-success/>

Brainyquotes. Retrieved Feb 2019.
<https://www.brainyquote.com/authors/benjamin-e-mays-quotes>

Genius. Retrieved Feb 2019.
<https://genius.com/Machine-gun-kelly-x-ambassadors-and-bebe-rexha-home-lyrics>

Retrieved Feb 2019
<http://2020co.s3.amazonaws.com/my2020portal/Flight+1.htm>

Goodreads. Retrieved March 2019
<https://www.goodreads.com/quotes/4353-the-ultimate-measure-of-a-man-is-not-where-he>

"Man In The Mirror" - written and composed by Siedah Garrett and Glen Ballard. Retrieved March 2019
<https://www.michaeljackson.com/track/man-mirror/>

MLive. Retrieved March 2019
<https://www.mlive.com/news/grand-rapids/2016/12/michigan_tech_defends_expulsio.html>

Dana Ford, CNN. Retrieved April 2019
<https://www.cnn.com/2015/11/09/us/jonathan-butler-hunger-strike-missouri-profile/index.html>

Frances Robles and Julie Bosman. August 2014. New York Times. Retrieved April 2019
<https://www.nytimes.com/2014/08/18/us/michael-brown-autopsy-shows-he-was-shot-at-least-6-times.html>

Made in the USA
Coppell, TX
12 March 2020